Favorite Poems

of Herbert Windolf

**Publications by Herbert Windolf,
As Translator of Karl May**

Published by Washington State University Press:
The Oil Prince

Published through BookSurge:
Black Mustang
with Marlies Bugman

Published by Nemsi Books:
The Treasure of Silver Lake
The Ghost of Llano Estacado
The Son of the Bear Hunter
Imaginary Journeys I
Imaginary Journeys II
Imaginary Journeys III
Thoughts of Heaven
Winnetou IV
Pacific Shores
The Inca's Legacy
The Scout
Deadly Dust
The Mahdi I

Published through CreateSpace:
The Mahdi II
The Mahdi III
One More Day . . .
As Translator of Autobiography of Isabell Steiner

As Author of Poetic Prose:
Through Booksurge:
Observations and Reflections
Pondering What Is
Otherwise
Musings
Contemplations

Through Kindle Direct Publishing:
Thoughts
Searching
Shadows and Light
Insights

Private Printing:
Biography – Bridges Across Times and Continents

Published by Verlag für Tiefenpsychologie und Anthropologie:
Brücken über Zeiten und Kontinente,
Biography – with Dorothea Rutkowsky

Planetary Studies Foundation Quarterly
Travelogues:
A Hike in Provence
A Safari Through Namibia
Alaska, the Last Terrestrial Frontier of the US
Galápagos
Excursions in Saxony's Switzerland
Monumental Sights, in Grand Staircase/Escalante, Utah, and
Northernmost Arizona
Journey to Sumatra
Zambezi
Moroccan Impressions
The Lure of Africa
Tanzania Redux, unpublished

Planetary Studies Foundation Quarterly
Ten Explorations, six published:
The likely Futility of S.E.T.I. Programs
Snowball Earth
Wondrous Water
The Probability for Intelligent Life in the Universe
A Personal View of Existentialism
Tsunami
Pragmatism
Forty billion Potentially Habitable Planets
Exceptionalism
December 26, 1776

Annemarie Schnitt - Willkommen Website
Translations of Poems and Stories

Unpublished – for Private Use
Autobiography
Translations:
The Texas War of Independence in 1836
by Herman Ehrenberg
Five Years Behind Barbed Wire
by Walter Hartmann
Letters to David Walter
Heinrich Himmler, by Franz Wegener
Ukraine Letters, by Hans Windolf
Germany's Final Months of WWII, Diary of Hans Windolf
The Forgotten Generation, by Sabine Bode
War's Grandchildren, by Sabine Bode
Genesis, by Dorothea Rutkowsky

Courses facilitated:
From the Spice Trade to Globalization
Cataclysms and Extinctions
The Likely Futility of SETI Programs
The Cambrian Explosion
Human Evolution and Migration
The American National Mind vis-à-vis the Rest of the World

Addendum
in *Thoughts*
A Collection of Haiku Verses
in *Searching*
Three African Stories
in *Shadows and Light*
Ten Explorations
in *Insights*
Comments &Autobiography
in *Favorite Poems*
Fourteen Travelogues

Introduction

Favorite Poems

Table of Contents

Table of Contents

Table of Contents   **Page:**

Travelogues

Introduction

Thus, in the year 2021 CE, the third year of the Covid-19 pandemic, I, once more thought to have finally come to the end of my writing of prosetry, my poetic prose, as I've come to call it, cheek in tongue. But then I wrote for a future volume #11: "I must write or I will die."

Through the years I may have concocted, more or less, one thousand seven hundred poems, now heading for two thousand. I have lost count since some of my poems take up, although rarely, more than one page.

I could also add, what I call, several hundred ditties, which I've written for birthdays and special occasions. And, last but not least, there are the hundreds of German poems which I have translated into the American language.

I have self-published – who would buy my stuff – nine volumes of prosetry, foremost for myself, but also to entertain or harass my fellow beings. Thus, the thought occurred to me to peruse all my poems and select my Favorites in a tenth volume. Going through them, my meandering of several decades, I realized that I, at times, addressed the same subject, but usually in a somewhat different manner.

I could have included a few more titles of my poetic prose but did not want to dilute my selection. I noticed the extent to which I favored my nature-related stories, and humorous skits, resulting in fewer of my philosophical comments. But, as I've claimed in one of my poems: "What comes from the so-called heart is usually better than what springs from the mind."

Finally, I have included fourteen travelogues as a supplement. Plenty more trips, excursions, travels, journeys, and safaris took place which I did not choose to write about.

Herbert Windolf   Prescott, AZ

Love

Quand serat-il
le cri des mouettes
das Spiel des Windes
wie Finger in deinem Haar
a whispering of trees:
je t'aime
ein Wissen der Trauben
je te bois
Arme - golden I'm Sonnenlicht
Sterne
toi et moi
here or anywhere
jamais - une foi - ou toujours?

Belonging

I am – born German
At home in America
yet at heart European
By intellect Western Man
Human by species
Member of all life by evolution
Part of the universe by chemistry

Farewell

Now that my consciousness depart'd forever
I wish to tell you, here and now:
How much I loved you, Ute, Dearest,
but now it's time to say good bye.
In a hundred years I'll be forgotten,
and that is how it well should be,
so many others came before,
at best, I'll be a mark on the family tree.
If soul possessed me –
now gone for good –
will it linger for a while in thee?
In the hereabouts, life's deeds committed,
they had their meaning as they should.
I wish you well for years to come,
live happily and fill your life.
And when it comes to our failings:
So what! Did we not try the best we could?
I did my "things" through joy and strife,
with some regrets, as I surely should!
You stuck with me through "thick and thin,"
and in the end – lo – did we win!
But, may I tell you now in closing:
Could I have had a better wife!

Ephemeral

White does it shimmer from up north,
once more are glaciers walking forth.
The land below, still, oh so green,
soon will be losing all its sheen.
Deer, bison, elk will move down south,
bear, wolf and other creatures in their wake.
But what of man, his proud creations,
will stand against the onslaught, when
the mass of ice will grind to dust
what to the mountains it has done.
Woe to us humans – ephemeral –
not knowing, oh, how frail we are!
We will be shattered and be driven
into an unimaginable land afar.

Beauty

What I will miss, when I'll be going,
will be the beauty of this Earth!
The harshness of her desert countries,
the richness of her vales,
her shores, her rivers and her lakes,
not to forget the life she bears.
So, what I've done throughout my life,
I journeyed far and wide,
took in her beauty where I found it,
across her seas and lands.
Her lakes and forests, up in Sweden,
which took me to Canadian shores;
from there to Caribbean isles
and to Galapagos, in time.
My true love, though, was Africa,
from where my ancestors bore forth,
the richness of her animal life,
which so intrigued me early on,
caused me to travel, when just twenty,
to Libya and Egypt's lore,
then to Morocco – and some more.

Stood on the plains of Serengeti and crossed Ngorongoro,
saw Moon and Venus light reflect
from her Zambezi's waters,
saw them becoming Smoke-That-Thunders,
known better as Victoria Falls.
Three days I canoed the Zambezi, like I had done before
in Minnesota and Ontario.
There was Namibia's rugged land,
the richness of the Okavango, the harshness of the
Kalahari,
and a Botswana, Zimbabwe and Zambia safari.
I swam the waters of Lake Toba,
sailed the lagoon of Bora Bora.
The verdant fields of my home country –
so beautiful – brought forth some tears;
and what delight it was to see
the west coast of America.
Sequoias reaching for the heavens,
eagles cartwheeling from the sky.
The Tetons, grand, like Jackson Hole,
and north of it, the Yellowstone.

Once, the Alaskan fjords were calling,
her lands, her glaciers, wild her lives.
The mountains of New Zealand's south,
magnificent, like Doubtful Sound.
And Turkey's southern shores we sailed,
to see the ruins the ancients left.
There were the hikes in Burgundy, Provence and the
Alsace,
and in the Alps, these old and civil lands,
in Tuscany and Umbria, America, and thus.
Now, in the autumn of my life,
I find experience more close-by,
in wonderful geology, so many eons old,
laid down so near my final home, the magnificent
Southwest.
And come the day, if I am lucky,
there'll be a wind right strong and fast
to blow my ashes to their final rest.

Alive

They come in all sizes,
large, medium and small,
in many a color,
in boisterous shapes,
so bright and alive,
and I love them all!
So, what are you wond'ring,
my reading friend?
It's not what you think!
It's Zinnias, I meant.

Fairy Tales

When I was four, and dusk was settling,
my grandma took me on her lap.
She told me fairy tales galore,
for me to grow up with this lore.
In fairy tales all things can happen,
like magic, coming from a void.
Impressionable, as kids are,
I took it in, believed it all.
Feats the heroes did perform
came out of nowhere, as a norm.
No matter, physical or mental,
they happened on their beck and call!
I ran with it, made them my own,
subliminally believed it all.
Then, when I got into my teens,
I thought I had these very means,
to do, like magic, what I wanted,
at any time, at any call.
That tasks of physical and mental nature,
called for my nose to the grindstone,
I, by the hard way, had to learn;
it doesn't help to simply yearn.

Thus, in the many years to come,
I buckled down, worked, and then some.
But faintly, back, deep in my mind,
there's still that voice that whispers on,
that I can do whatever comes,
like magic, on my beck and call.

Wanted

We enter this life;
alone we are.
We seek the one,
who,
not just in part,
but as a whole,
is going to want us,
body and soul.

Holding Hands

In the night
she lies next to me.
I reach out with my open hand
and quickly hers comes touching mine,
probing, playing, firmly resting.
My fingers caress,
hers padding back.
What trust she extends
to me holding on.
In touch with another being,
we enjoy its pleasure.
I'm holding hands –
with a cat.

Supper

Canoeing the Zambezi River with our guide,
his young wife and some helpers
driving a trail by the river,
set up camp every night.
For three days we paddled,
passing hippos aplenty.
Each evening we found respite, a shower nearby.
One night was special,
forever to behold.
Not far from the river our table was set
with all the accouterments
of civilization one expects.
The mighty, gnarled tree
under which we dined lent character,
held civilization and the wilds entwined.
And on the waters moonlight reflected,
joined by a streak of Venus shine.
On the opposite bank a hyena cackled,
while we eleven in comfort dined.
Some people may see this in a different light,
that it was no adventure but "safari light."
Yet I remember it
as a magical night.

Big Sur

Breakers slam into waiting rocks,
their salty spray wetting my face.
Whistling, the wind blows spume apace.
Thundering waves from across the ocean,
once spent on the rocks,
leave naught a trace,
but are repeated night and day.
Out on the water kelp waves its fronds.
How deep do its stems reach down to the sand?
An otter securely tangled in kelp
floats on its back, and
with a pebble from the deep,
is busy cracking a mussel's shell.
A gull's hoarse cry is drifting by,
a flock of pelicans passes in silent array.
Aeons old, this image will last,
into a future, distant,
when Man is long past.

Lights

High in the night of the African sky,
magnificent, the Southern Cross.
Some distance away Venus shines brightly,
Jove cavorting around her day by day.
Fireflies dance through the night,
broad, the Rufiji River flows silently by.
At times a Tiger fish the surface breaks,
a croc produces a sudden splash.
Across the river hippos grunt,
a flock of birds, late, wing their way to roost.
Dark, the river's opposite bank,
not a single light there breaking the night
of the Selous Reserve in Tanzania's south.
Behind me the lights of the Sand River Resort,
ahead some of what is left of Africa's Wilds
that make do with only the lights in the sky.

Silence a

Oh how I cherish stillness, quiet,
the lack of sound,
the peace it brings.
Deeper thoughts rise to the surface
that otherwise are swamped by noise.
And comes the day there be eternal silence,
no longer thoughts troubled by ill.
At last the final peace it brings,
I'm certain of it,

yes,

it will.

To Touch Someone

by mind alone,
by reaching out
in open tone.
By giving of our very self
that which moves us
deep within.
To break the shell
of our prison,
expose the feelings
we hold back.
Free we become,
one with the other,
at least a bit
for while it lasts.
Physical, a touch may be,
but spiritual touch
is our apogee.

Loons

North, in the wilderness,
the call of the loon,
solitude amplified,
under a gibbous moon.
Haunting it sounds,
enticing, too.
Could I hear it forever,
become one with the wildness,
meld into her arms,
be gathered home.

There was a Time

----

when I walked the land,
my mate behind,
our cub on her arm.
I carry a club and check the wind,
for vultures circling means there may be a kill.
The savanna's grasses are high at this time,
hyenas or lions could hide nearby.
For me, down here, it is hard to tell,
but carnivore reek is easy to smell.
Vulnerable we are, out here in the open,
few acacias offer a quick retreat.
But we must cross this expanse
to the black line not far,
to find succor across in bushes and trees.
I must find water and food
for my cub and mate.
But the time's not yet right
to ponder my fate.

Silence, 6

precious as can be!
Escape the hubbub, just be me.
Sit on a rock, observe the world,
way in the distance someone speaks.
Some grass blades waving in the wind,
a squirrel, noiseless, makes a sprint.
A butterfly visits some blooms,
and through the trees a titmouse roams.
There is an insect buzzing past,
a single croak a raven calls.
Now, do not think this breaks the silence,
the peace and quiet I enjoy,
oh no, it all enhances silence,
it holds me spellbound, it enthralls!

Anger

be cursed when it flares up wild.
When sudden rage turns me into a child.
When the limbic system,
mood and emotion,
in the blink of an eye,
take control of the forebrain, the seat of reason.
Just as sudden the tempest will fade,
then what is left is remorse and shame.
But worse is the knowledge
that a future event
may trigger again the very same.
What dwells beneath this,
what is the reason?
Is it helplessness, a lack of control?
But the instant it does happen
means a loss of soul.
And the memory haunts forever on,
for nothing can undo
what in a moment was done.

Rational Spirituality

Is it possible, can it be,
can there exist such a duality?
Rational refers to reason and logic,
down-to-earth, pragmatic thought,
not what religion and mysticism have wrought.
Spirituality affects the human spirit, the soul,
defined here as the composite of mind,
as opposed to physical things of all kinds.
Is it not rational to care for, to love the world,
her oceans, mountains, rivers and lakes,
the creatures we share it with, our fellow-women and men,
knowing we're one with all that it holds?
Is it not rational to be optimistic despite
all the trouble we cause
to the detriment of the soul?
Are these rational thoughts, or spiritual, too?
Like knowing there's no certainty?
That whatever there is is probability?
To live with uncertainty,
be skeptical of all there is,
also trust in one's being,
knowing it is
rational spirituality.

Epitaph

When will it be?
The raven's croak,
a gust of wind to carry me,
home,
to wherever on this Earth
there's peace to find from this, my world
that slides away,
slips through my fingers day by day.
No longer pain of any kind,
again be one with
dust
which is
where I came from
before I grew,
developed mind.

Limerick

There once was this kid from a little town
who ventured into the world.
He tried and strove and in the end,
he thought he had it made.
But lo and behold,
when all was done,
he found he had after all failed.

Deliberateness

Dogs, so loyal,
are full of emotion.
Cats are deliberate,
they parse their devotion.

Flight

I crossed the Atlantic in business class;
on a Triple-7 was my flight.
Had champagne, all kinds of goodies, salad, a filet mignon,
and finished it with a sundae to boot.
Yet for more such pleasures I'd have not given a hoot.
There was one thing which would have made the setting
just right:
I'd have loved sitting next to me
the fellows who made this all possible:
Orville and Wilbur Wright.

Radiant

Young woman,
still in the blush of youth,
in the glow of first love,
radiant she is.

Africa

I have been to the deserts,
the Namib, the Sahara.
I've canoed the Zambezi,
crossed the plain of Amboseli.
Ballooned the Mara, chased hippos in that river,
had elephants chasing me in Botswana.
Seen ancient ruins most plentiful,
in Morocco, Libya, and Egypt.
Entered the Valley of Kings and Hatshepsut's temple
with my buddy, the only visitors there.
I have walked the bush in tow of a guide,
his rifle at the ready,
always wondering what the next thicket might hide.
I've seen giraffes, antelopes, crocs,
warthogs and lions galore,
elephants, buffalo, and many more,
seen them by daylight and in the night.
I've met and enjoyed
many people from near and afar.
Believe me, dear reader,
when I hold it dear and say here:
"There's always the call of Africa."

The Noise

In the stillness of night,
and in a restful day,
there is a noise
that keeps thumping away.
It sounds like the pistons
that drive a steamship.
For as long as there's fuel
for the fires to leap,
it propels the ship
against current and fate.
And come the day
when the fire burns down,
the ship runs aground,
the pumping heart
stops its sound.

Te Quiero

Am I right?
Is it true?
Am I really sure?
Can that which I seek
truly be found,
or is it just a lure
that keeps me suspended
to try forever, of course, in vain,
to find that which cannot be found,
only pain?
But I love the pursuit,
the horizon is close,
to continue the search,
for there must be one.

Fear of Dying

haunts the living.
Fear of consciousness, that is.
Fear of what they might find in Hell,
for few in Heaven will ever dwell.
What troubles most, however, is,
that there may lurk only nothingness.

The Bell

There came the time
when a pilgrim I was,
to a village in Würtemberg lands.
There, in the last year of the War,
I'd found peace from the dropping bombs.
First at seven, then eight in nineteen-forty-four,
I had had the run of the place.
One day, I recall, I was taken by elders
to the little village church.
They showed me how to pull the rope
to get the bell to ring,
and once I did, I rose to the heavens,
but ring the bell I did.
Again I stood in the little church,
likely a final time.
A guest book lay in front of me,
waiting for words of mine.
Signing it, I thought it well
to tell other readers that:
Seventy years ago,
I'd rung this very bell.

Travelers

I once met in Cairo a German nurse
who was on her way to Kenya.
There she expected to inherit a farm,
I met others like her. Hallelujah!
She had pedaled from Berlin
all the way to Morocc'
then along the North African coast.
In Cairo we were for three weeks stuck,
since Brits and French had Egypt struck.
The woman was fifty but firm on foot.
One day she offered to darn my socks.
A worldly, older friend – I was twenty – suggested:
Herb, she's after more, watch her, she rocks.
She pedaled to Aswan and back to Cairo,
refused entry into Sudan.
She just wasn't prepared by the fellahin official
to be bedded for a visa she didn't have.
My buddy and I then split in Cairo,
I went home while he gave it a further go.
Later I heard to Ethiopia he got
with the rocking nurse
who was darning his socks.

Svelte

Summertime, oh summertime,
when you see lightly clad runners
striving to stay trim and fine.
It is a pleasure to see fluidity and grace,
good proportions, height, and poise.
And with a ponytail tossing in the breeze,
aesthetics is complete.
A little sex, too,
about which there is nothing to sneeze.

Soul

No, not the ethereal, immortal kind,
but the totality of body and mind.
The lifetime sensations experienced
by intellect and physique,
the joys and pains
that make a person unique.
The time to wonder an individual took,
to see, hear, smell, and learn
not just learn by the book.
This, altogether, even more than that
will, with compassion and feeling,
maybe result in the fullness of being.

Rivulets

Minuscule, a foot maybe wide,
meandering through meadows
of ancient times.
I recall them from childhood,
trout swimming in them,
the water clear and shimmering.
The image lingers in my mind.
Oh, could I only return
to the clarity of this time.

Gaia

I am born of this planet,
I am part of it.
With its peace and its fury,
its starkness and beauty,
it is me, I am it.
I am part of Gaia's mountains,
her deserts and seas,
her forests and rivers,
and all life she bears.
I am her Mind,
who, aware, sees and feels.
Through fellow-sentients and me
Gaia becomes conscious,
an alive entity.
We are her mind,
her spirit, her soul.
Let us hope that this Mind
will continue to grow,
to take in and cherish
that of which we are a part,
but which we don't own.

Mind Bridge

How often have I wished to bridge the gulf
that separates my mind from that of my cats,
a raven, a dog, a porpoise, a wolf.
It includes all creatures large and small,
but not the human animal.
What do they feel, what do they think,
what's on the mind of a pig to be slaughtered,
what on a whale's, beached, its life on the brink?
How great a mystery are these hidden minds.
Will we ever be able to access their kinds?
Were I able to accomplish this wondrous feat,
not by Mephisto's unwanted deceit,
for to do so would rather be a god-given treat.
I would gladly give a year of my life,
to build a mind bridge, bold,
comprehending animals' souls.

Buddy

Spunky, my Buddy, I miss you so much!
Your company, your trust, your oft gentle touch.
You found me at home when your need was such.
Independent you were, with a character great.
We were a twosome, the two of us were!
It does not feel right to push you away,
in my mind that is, for my tears to stay.
Now you lie in your grave
under stones heavy and cold.
Spunky, oh Spunky, why did you have to grow old.
I know you had to leave after eighteen long years,
but it does not prevent my occasional tears.
I do miss you, dear cat.
If only, once more, I could love and behold you,
enjoy your trust and your gentle touch.
Spunky, my Buddy, I miss you so much!

Encore

When love is lost,
can it rise once more,
from ashes abundant
to a triumphant encore?

Tic-toc

Thus time went by.
Sitting in the stillness of night,
waiting for the siren's final cry,
that told of needing to seek shelter,
or, relieved, go to bed again, sleepy-eyed.
Thus, still today,
in the quiet of night,
when I hear this sound,
it tells me how and why
time goes by.
Tic-toc.

Buck

There is this buck who
walks through my yard
and, of course, my neighborhood too.
I love to watch him,
always alert,
his face so lovely, so very pert.
Could I only step out
to give him a hug,
and tell him: I love you,
but our worlds are apart.
We cannot find peace
which once was a given
in paradise.

Pelicans

They look like a leftover from the Cretaceous,
in flight they do not look very gracious.
But, oh, when the Browns go diving for fish,
streak for the water with great panache.
I've often identified with this bird,
it's awkwardness in flight,
yet it's dive into water
so daring, so great.
Only gannets are better at it,
but then, they are sleeker,
which helps quite a bit.

Forgiving

Trying to remember life's take and give,
oddly, I do not recall anything,
I have need to forgive.
Is this because no one did me wrong,
or, when it happened,
the hurt did not linger,
but was quickly gone.
It does not pay to carry along
a pain, an injury ere been done.
Did I simply shrug off every insult and wrong,
shucks, I'm free,
or is my memory gone?

Mind-Meld 2

It is only today that I realized
the always-having-been-present
desire to enter other minds.
Not just the obvious human kinds,
but also of fellow-creatures that come to mind.
To plumb their depths,
to fathom what makes them tick,
to understand and come closer bit by bit.
And in this coming-closer, yet to build,
a unity to be fulfilled.
I haven't yet found the cause of this wish,
but may still have some time
to probe for the source of it.

Chrysalis

A quiescent pupa, what marvel it is,
a butterfly in waiting to escape its confine,
to spread its wings and soar to the sky,
to flutter here and there,
a joy to the eye.
Humans too, a chrysalis can be,
enclosed in their shell,
unable to break free.
Oh, if only they could fracture their confining shell,
soar too to the heavens,
break their hindering spell,
and release the beauty
which inside them dwells.

Somebody Home

From time to time
one sees a face
which looks alive
has depth and grace.
And instantly, like a living poem,
I know, I know,
there's somebody home.

Outsider,

I've been at the best of times.
Insider when I write my rhymes.
Haunted by this "standing aside,"
when others had fun,
I wasn't along for the ride.
There's always this sense
that I do not belong,
that I'm somehow different,
that something is wrong.
Even when among friends
it makes for a lonely
individualistic stance,
in life's ever so complex dance.

Pressure Differential

There was this good lady,
short of some ink,
for her Brother printer it was, I think?
It was black that was called for,
by no means pink.
She pulled the tab on the cartridge as told,
but the "bullet's" charge had been placed
close to sea level's hold.
Prescott, my hometown, is a mile or more high,
and without warning, it caught her cold.
The accident was a horrid mess,
but before all was done she looked as if
she had tried to make love to an octopus.

Redeemstress

I wonder why the Christian God
didn't dispatch His daughter
to redeem humanity's lot?

I Am Who I Am

When Moses descended the mountain
with the tablets he'd been handed,
he called up for the giver's name?
And a voice he supposedly heard from above, said
"I Am Who I Am."
I, too, make this claim
from where I have come
and to where's now my aim.

Thoughts

Blown in the wind,
like milkweed seed pods,
Monarch butterfly food,
ephemeral, come today,
defined, refined, gone in a spin.

Tails

Some are short, some bushy,
some long, some are tall.
They help their owners keep balance,
prevent a fall.
Humans, without one,
have no balance at all.

Grebes

They walk the water with power and grace.
Have you ever seen them perform their mating dance?
In unison they move their heads,
sideways, looking left and right,
swiftly, then again each other they face,
all the while walking their beautiful prance.
A supreme enjoyment it is to watch them dance.
Here and there you may have heard some talk,
but it's not only humans who on water can walk.

Albacore

Today I prepared a salad for lunch,
with red pepper, onion, pickle, and tomato,
not to forget salt, pepper, lemon juice and mayo,
and as its base the flesh of tuna.
You were spawned an Albacore
and survived predation to grow.
Then schooled in Pacific tropical waters,
a predator yourself you went with the flow
cruising the deep blue waters below.
Above, other predators cast the nets-of-man,
caught, you saw the light of day.
I think of you, fish!
Even when for me to eat
you ended up in a metal can.

Overreach

it was, I wanted,
and I want it still today.
Reach the other, mind to mind,
at times, when both are so inclined.
To feel the other's deepest thoughts,
to share mine, understand directly,
spared the common verbal onslaught,
which, slow, deals in metaphors, in similes,
trying to describe what's felt,
and struggles with analogies,
words, in which the rational mind dwells.
This overreach can't come to pass,
I know, I know, I'm stuck with molasses,
or brittle, inaccurate verbal glass,
used to describe what is felt, what is.
I know, I know, for I failed in this way,
which is why I wish for this overreach
to miraculously access directness,
still, to this day.

Birdbath

Commonly called thus,
the name's not quite true.
Birds do bathe in them
but more often they drink.
Trust me, this is what they do.
There is this nice neighbor
with a fancy bath of glass.
The bowl is quite deep,
with its edge hard to grasp.
Thus its purpose is defeated
to drink or to bathe.
The setup is nice,
but "it is for the birds."

You,

----

the one I love,
but who seeks distance between us.
You, with whom I feel at home,
no other comes close.
You, I have need for in my final years,
if only to reminisce
about the good things we shared.
You, who have need
from the shadows to rise
to leave the world of the Bad behind,
to yet grow and find your very self.
You, like me, learning
to express what we need
for a final beginning,
if ever again we are able to meet.
You, to find the strength
to forgive, not forget.
You, to find all that you seek,
and more of it yet.
All this before it is too late.

Cat

There, right in front of me,
in the middle of my desk,
blissfully, lies my cat at rest.
Not even a twitch of the tail she makes.
I do not dare leave,
for it's my company she craves.
Might I be able to rise, go fetch my book,
to return in time,
might this get me off the hook?
What all one does
for a creature one loves!

More Thoughts

What I like to do, too,
pardon, if I may,
is to stir up
the run-of-the-mill thoughts
of the run-of-the-mill day.
To entertain something different,
thoughts out of the way.
Sincerely, I hope, I succeed here and there.
If not, it's my fault,
my thoughts were elsewhere.

Literal

I've tried to write fiction,
but hard as I might,
nothing was worth reading.
I'm just too literal a guy.

Namib

We once passed through this desert the oldest in the world.
Our young guide, Kobus Pienaar, grown up on a farm,
told of his grandfather's right
to shoot a trespassing Bushman on sight.
Yet, he himself, with a Bushman as guide,
had roamed the veldt
to take in the lore his guide's country held.
There came a day when the three of us stopped
at a massive sandstone outcrop
in the middle of nowhere
for our midday repast.
When done I clambered up the broken rocks,
a bronze plaque suddenly made me stop.
Securely fastened,
it wasn't large, held just a name and dates,
and a small rock bowl next to it
held the person's remains,
the ashes the wind had not yet blown across the land.
What a marvelous place to find one's last rest.
The view, magnificent it was,
a memorial extraordinary,
his or her soulmate's bequest.

Existence

When I confront friends with the statement
that a rock does not exist
until it has been described and named,
they think I am nuts, maybe deranged.
Narrowly focused on the physical existence of the rock,
they fail to understand the power of language,
without which our world could be a void,
mentally blocked.
Any subject, physical or mental, real and alive,
is unknown to a language
until it is named, understood, described,
incorporated into a culture's life.
This is to say our world, all we describe,
is a construct.
Even the scientific method,
our pantheons of gods,
are existing only
for as long as we believe in these, our constructs,
until such time we leave them behind.

Driven a

I am to do what I must,
to acquire, to integrate in the time given,
myself, my being, to ever last,
before it's too late, before time has passed.
I sense the contradictions, yet the unity, too.
How will I be able to reconcile the two?
Strive I will, I know I am close,
yet there is still this distance,
somehow, somewhere, interposed.
I must do it myself, I'm at it alone,
a lifetime of folly must still be shed,
so much overblown, so deeply anchored
in the soul.

... and Yet, and Yet,

---

to just be, simply be,
at peace, having found equanimity,
not by setting a goal
but arising from the depth of the soul,
a Taoist distance, a rest in oneself,
letting go, yet being engaged in every sense.
Not an itch to scratch,
but with awareness high,
this would be the state I wish to achieve
before I depart, before I die.

Heartfelt Wish

May you not, at the end of your life,
be troubled by what was not to be,
but rather have arrived at the point
where you accept yourself and others
like a flowing windblown saree.
To enter the nothingness clean without guilt
with only love attached to your hilt.

Sharing

I am part of the minds of mice and men,
of the fishes in the deep blue sea,
of reptiles, insects, birds, and such,
of all the creatures that crawl, and fly,
and the gamut of microbial fry.
Of the waters, the air, the rocks, the volcanoes,
even earthquakes, bye-and-bye,
all part of Earth's life, her vibrant being,
giving and taking as she may.

Humor

The last thing, I guess, to which I'll acquiesce,
not reluctantly, and without protest, will be
my sense of humor, to reflect and to tease,
with the people about me,
the doctors and nurses,
the friends and family, as may be.
Humor, at root, covers the sadness of the world.
But for as long as I succeed
to light up a smile or bring a laugh to a face,
just for this very moment,
I brought joy apace.
What better way is there to leave this space?

Being One

Back, as far as I can think,
I wanted to be one with Everything.
To enter into the essence of all there is,
to comprehend how it works,
to understand how it feels,
to become one with the gamut of life
even its rocks immobile.
Not facile emotion I was looking for
but the empathy,
the acquisition of penetrating oneness,
to grow beyond the limited being of so much of life,
to become one, being one,
with all there is,
as I had sensed it in passing
at age seventeen,
standing at this Swedish quay,
singing into the wind and the sea.

Sighting

To what extent can we truly feel the pain,
the suffering of a fellow being?
Is it not usually at a distance perceived,
intellectualized, its true nature concealed?
Thus we only sight the pain
but rarely, if ever, engage the limbic system,
by which we feel, not merely see.
Just like two ships sighting each other passing
in a fog at sea.

Foibles

I love to mock this human trait,
the many foibles which are our fate.
Most are minor and personal flaws.
Others, more general,
can get stuck in your craw.
Thus I enjoy in some of my prose
to tease and to taunt,
knowing full well
that I'm part of the crowd.

Probabilistic

Neither am I a theist who believes in God,
considering His existence as true,
which many people would swear to know,
nor an atheist
denying His existence as fraud.
Both cannot know from observation
what is truly true,
but are forever beholden
by whatever story they were told.
Nothing in the world we know
can ever be totally certain,
only probably so.
Thus I'm content to live
with this smidgen of uncertainty
of a deity's existence
and the knowledge of the universe
at its today's veriest,
making me a probabilistic atheist.

Loner

For much of my life a loner I have been,
an introvert, a spiritual nonconformist,
an outsider, whatever that means.
From my early years I've felt
that somehow I didn't fit in,
and, come to think of it,
had no desire to give it a spin.
What early on did drive me on
was to be my very own man.
I think I succeeded,
and when I look at my recent pics,
I am content with what they depict.

Sights and Sounds

Clouds drifting across the sky,
a rainbow rising high,
a motorcycle's noisy roar,
a pair of turkey vultures soar,
a phone ringing next door,
the song of birds, my cat's meow,
the scent of falling rain,
a starry night, the day's breaking light,
the bark of dogs,
a distant fire engine's wail,
wispy contrails of a plane,
a lunch date to share,
cavorting in the sky a raven pair,
two bucks passing through the yard,
the setting sun a glorious reward,
wind whooshing through trees,
the buzz of bees,
wind chimes tinkling,
the laugh of a woman
on the street with others mingling.
Sights and sounds,
ephemeral memoirs,
just as all loves and sorrows are.

Pursuable Entity

There is this young lady
of three-score-and-ten years,
slender, of good face,
and a demeanor to please.
Too bad she's not free,
so this is a tease.
If I were younger, unencumbered,
in good health, and without blight,
well, I'd give it a shot,
just for good company and what not,
and here and there a hug and a squeeze,
if that's alright.
All this, provided she too would agree,
she'd sure be a pursuable entity.

Dream

Again and again, the dream recurs,
to leave the hubbub
of the contemporary world.
But not quite yet,
there's still much to be observed.
It being early September,
the mosquitoes have taken a break.
To sit in peace by the shore
of a small Canadian lake.
Gaze across its placid waters,
dusk settling at a rising moon.
The shimmer of its light,
a silver spoon.
A single-malt Scotch, neat,
its bouquet, not only, a pleasant treat.
A good friend nearby
with whom to trade a kind word, by and by.
Listening to the silence
and the haunting calls of a loon.

Sui Generis

Rational to a high degree,
which is why I claim to be sui generis.

Reflections

The fire is burning lower.
Embers glow in the dark.
Thoughts arise of what all I've committed,
and where I've left my mark.
Where I have failed,
what I have learned,
where I've succeeded,
where I got burned.
There's the age-old thought:
"If only I could go back,
and right the wrongs
for a better track."
But as it happens,
without mistakes,
we wouldn't learn,
belatedly,
what it truly takes.

Pillow

My arms rests on a pillow
elaborately stitched.
It once came from India,
bought by my gone sister-in-law.
The years have caused it to fade a bit,
but I often wondered of who stitched it?
It was likely a woman,
poor as a mouse,
who worked for a wage
not enough for life.
Many times have I thought:
I'd love to meet her,
to tell how I admire her work.
But most likely she's long gone,
to where no pillows are made.

Innocence

There is this story of the Garden of Eden,
where the first human beings lived,
innocent, like animals,
not knowing the difference
between good and bad.
Then, when we ate
from the Apple of Knowledge,
when we became conscious,
the world forever changed.
I am no believer of stories,
but this one is as good as it gets.

Loki

My psycho-friend Norm
honored me today
by applying a, what he thought appropriate,
nickname to me,
Loki,
the Trickster god of Norse mythology.
That's as close as I come, god-like to be.
Norm thinks that I'm playing this game,
twisting and teasing without shame.
Come to think, I realize now,
why I am fond of the coyote,
the Indian trickster of fame.
Ah, why not have a little fun in life
and proudly carry Loki's name.
Yet, I need to watch out,
Loki ended when to a rock he was bound.

Bananas

You may recall, I told before,
I've provisioned myself
to have enough food and goodies
to last me in isolation four months or more.
However, all by myself, nuts I might go,
and if that's not enough, bananas too.
But I'll try to make the best of it,
at the end of my driveway open a stand,
where I will sell at a distance of six feet,
whatever's in stock, what I have on hand.
And should I run out of bananas, shucks,
I can always switch over to hawking nuts.

Infinity

I sit on a boulder in my yard,
Rikki behind me exploring her world.
Conscious awareness is mine while it lasts.
The wind sings to me in the bushes and trees,
a bouquet of yellow flowers grows next to my feet.
All this must end, no more sensations,
no longer being of this world, no more observations.
Yet I can't help imagining what all I have been,
what my molecules, my elements have already seen.
Did some trod the Earth in a triceratops,
and before grace a carboniferous fern?
What will yet happen to my few remains?
The biome of my very Self
will, too, go the way of all earthly things,
expire in the flames the fire will bring.
But then,
somewhere away from the rush of the world,
my ashes will be dispersed by the wind,
rain will wash some into the earth.
Will my molecules, my atoms, my elements,
nourish yet other beings in life's marvelous sea,
a nematode in the soil, a leaf on a tree?

Will a browsing doe's milk feed her fawn yet to be?
Might I grace the world in a flower's bloom?
Lucky me if a tree's roots take me in
and in a juniper I live for a few hundred years.
I shall be recycled, it's nature's design,
in the Earth, in Life, engulfed by the sun.
I am infinite.
Infinity is mine.

Kindred Spirit

Rarely does one find,
as one saunters through life,
a woman or man
- oh, what a joy it is -
who dare bare their mind,
to stand naked before you,
yet never lose the dignity of their
spirit, their soul.
Kindred they are,
one of a kind.

Tao

It's claimed the Tao cannot be defined,
but may I try it after all?
I came across this statement, that of the Tao te Ching:
"When the Tao is lost there is Goodness,
When Goodness is lost there is Kindness,
When Kindness is lost there is Justice.
When Justice is lost there is Ritual.
Ritual is the Husk of Faith and Hope
and the Beginning of Chaos."
So, while it does not mention Love,
it covers quite a bit.
It's deeper than it seems to be,
what might it mean, what might be it?
What is it for the seeing?
Dare we to claim yet after all:
The Fullness of our Being!

Reinforcement

It's not impossible, but maybe,
I discovered how people maintain their ideology.
They mouth it at every opportunity.

Catamount

Once more the earlier morning sun
has called me to my favorite boulder,
RikkiCat having her daily run.
Between sips of coffee I close my eyes,
enjoying the precious morning quiet.
A faint noise causes me to look up,
and there, a few feet away,
looking straight at me, sits this puma cat.
There is not threat in her demeanor,
just cautious appraisal by this creature.
I have no fear with this mountain lion so near.
We seem to commune a sense of belonging,
a sense of being one with the world we share.
A squeeze of her eyes, a final goodbye,
and she fades away in the blink of an eye.
Did I imagine her? Was she real?
I truly can't say.

Pictures

I have been on several safaris.
My wife took pictures.
I did not.
In Tanzania, five years ago,
on my solo last safari,
I didn't take a single shot.
I looked, I saw, I remember, I forgot.

Ode to Birds

I love and admire all these birds,
most in nature I observed.
There is the gannet with its diving panache
the brown pelican for its headlong dash
the loon with its haunting voice
ravens cavorting in the sky
smart crows with their raucous cries
the puffins, painted clowns of the seas
mourning doves pursuing mates
the eagle for its soaring might
humming birds in their fancy flight
the bushtits flitting through the trees
minor goldfinches going for thistle seed
owls hooting in the early morn
phainopeplas catching insects in the sky
a Cooper hawk dashing for its prey
the road runner for its funny gait
the turkey vulture for its circling flight
the blue jay chasing other birds away
house finches in their plenitude

the grosbeaks for their plump demeanor
towhees in their seed pursuit
lazuli buntings passing through
penguins flying through the water
blue-footed boobies in their mating dance
grebes of their walking-on-water prance
the albatross on its epic journeys
ostriches running across the veldt
bee eaters in their loamy burrows
a red-wing blackbird, companion for a few days
a meadow lark singing her life away in the sky
queleas flocking in the thousands
cranes stalking their prey in the shallows
the secretary bird hunting in the grass
gulls, always hungry, everywhere
lilac-breasted rollers in their fancy dress
king fishers catching a fish in a dash
weaver birds in their copious nests
kori bustards, with their funny name
storks building their high-up nests
parrots, gorgeous in flight and at rest
nightingales singing sweetly at dusk

ducks in their many kinds
storks rattling along the Rhine
oxpeckers pecking for insects and blood
flickers hammering on the boards of the house
robins bobbing in their search for worms
titmice coming for a grain at a time
the peregrine falcon in its headlong dive
cranes flying straight-necked in the sky
geese for V-formation try
starlings in fantastic murmurations
frigates, thieving in the skies
the dipper diving for tidbits in a stream
quails with their wailing call
a kookaburra alighting on a rail
the wren twittering here and there
condors soaring high in the air
cormorants diving for their food
cardinals, bright red in their suit
cassowaries to avoid
cuckoos calling in Tuscan woods
pigeons out for their daily food
a waxwing flock raiding my pyracantha bush

guinea hens flocking through the brush
nuthatches climbing trees
the plenitude of birds-of-paradise
Galapagos finches in their variety.
All this evolution has wrought
from dinosaurs to today's multitude.

Imaginings

More and more, as days go by,
the errors I make multiply,
the body, too, is no longer spry.
After breakfast my RikkiCat waits
to venture to the yard with me.
While she observes, explores her world,
I sit on my favorite boulder,
sipping from my emptying cup.
I watch the dappling of the rising sun,
a light breeze caresses my face.
Closing my eyes, the silence, an embrace.
A gentle tap on my shoulder. I look up,
There, next to me, lo,
stands this ghostly figure telling me softly:
"Come. It is time to go."

Anticipating

I've followed this motto for most of my life,
to think ahead to what may arrive.
Nothing's assured the way we expect,
it may not suffice to merely react.
That's why I didn't operate blind,
rather followed my motto below:
"If I'm not ahead, I will be behind."

Flirting with Death

Friends urge me not to dwell on my demise,
that another day is yet to rise.
Yes it will, one more affliction to bring.
One more to eventually do me in.
Thus I write here and there
that soon I will go.
I tease the Rim Greaper
for whatever it's worth.
That's why it is called:
Flirting with death.

Intimate

My psycho-friend Norm,
my most intimate friend,
has come up with a Comment.
Short as it is, it is very well penned.
In many a conversation we probed existence,
from the simple to the grand.
He knows what he's saying,
becoming socratic, even wise.
His Comment is brief:
"Herbert lives the examined life."

Anthropos

No matter his or her color,
no mater where they are from,
what matters is competence
and more so good will.

Driven 6

Once I had outgrown my dormant pre-teens,
I aimed to excel in life's multifarious scenes.
Dynamic, I went for what I took into sight.
I was tops in drafting,
sold goods to make a buck,
and itched to travel,
which took me to Scandinavia,
Africa, France, Spain, and back.
I gained a wife, three children too,
had a well-paying job,
but longed to see more of the world.
With the consent of my wife
Canada called, then the United States.
I survived the discharge of my colleagues,
fell up the ladder as managing director,
to rebuilt the company in the coming years.
Through tumultuous times I stayed engaged,
eventually importing and selling myself.

A dining group I kept on track,
just as I did with another discussing
what makes the world tick.
I translated and wrote many a work,
in due course, in American language I excelled
but, by now, I have come to the end.
Success came my way,
I worked for it.
Driven, I was,
and I payed for it,
in issues of health,
and the wife I beheld.

Epiphany

At seventeen I was in Sweden,
stood on a jetty, facing west.
The sun was setting, wind was blowing,
the sea was rough – I was at rest!
I stood there for the longest time
and sang into the wind.
Then, more and more, something did happen,
wide open did become my mind.
So wide that it included all,
while I was every part of it.
I was the world, the world was I,
this, what my spirit now beheld.
A feeling was it – wonderful –
too difficult for me to tell.
How did it happen, came to being?
Much later did I understand.
It was the setting and my singing,
which so enchanted and entranced
and took me to this far-off land!

"Yeah, my soul went free, and, wheeling like an eagle,
I saw indeed that there was no Teshoo Lama,
nor any other soul.
As a drop draws to water, so my soul drew near
to the Great Soul which is beyond all Hind,
from Ceylon in the sea to the Hills,
and my own painted rock at Such-zen;
I saw evert camp and village, to the least,
were we have ever rested.
I saw them at one time and in one place;
for they were within the soul.
By this I knew the soul had passed beyond
the illusion of time and space and of things.
By this I knew that I was free."
Rudyard Kipling, Kim

The Lure of Africa

Written in 2011

As of today, I have made seven trips to Africa and have written travelogues on several. It being highly unlikely that I will be off on an eight's venture, allow me to travel back in time, more than five decades, to write about my first trip to the 'Dark Continent.' Since childhood, when I began to read, and was fascinated by the German colonial exploits in east and southwest Africa, this continent exerted a peculiar fascination on me.

When I had reached 19, having traveled a bit in Germany and twice to Sweden, with my life unsettled, not knowing where to go, I hit on the idea of bicycling solo around the globe. My parents vetoed this thought. Then I came up with buying a motorcycle, attach a side car to it, find a companion, and travel from Germany via north and east Africa to Cape Town, there to hire on on a steamer to return home, but it took more than 20 years for me to, eventually, make it to that city. Back then, I saved and saved my salary for this venture and sold all kinds of things to my colleagues in the design department I was working at, eventually acquiring about 3,000 deutschmarks. I found an age-mate to join me and eventually purchased that motorcycle rig. A solid hinged steel lid with a padlock covered the opening of the sidecar to protect our travel gear; the intention was for us to ride on the cycle back-to- back. A 20 liter gasoline tank was strapped to the outside.

A few days after my 20th birthday, the beginning of October 1956, we set off, me after a week's earlier extraction of a molar. We headed south and stopped at the D.K.W. factory for a refurbishing of my vehicle, and had to spend more than had been budgeted. We did not carry cold-weather clothing and on our drive through the Alps, even through northern Italy, we came close to freeze our derrieres off. Oh, what a relief it was when, at last, we exited a road tunnel that opened to the warm breezes of the Mediterranean Sea. Down the 'boot' we drove, along the Amalfi coast to Naples, where we boarded an Italian steamer to take us to Tripoli in Libya. This was when King Idris still governed there, which makes me 'older' than Colonel Gaddafi, the usurper.

On the ship, we quickly became friends with a group of four, an about 30 year old German with his French wife, and their two, about 22 year old German traveling companions, all riding in a small Fiat car. The couple was, as they told, on their way to accept the inheritance of a Kenyan farm. Arriving in Tripoli in the afternoon, we made every effort to get out of the city into open country where we could camp. Alas, the date palm groves stretched east for mile after mile, and we had to camp off the road in a palm grove. Shacks nearby caused us five males to share guard duty through the night. One of the two younger fellows picked up and ate the dropping dates – and suffered from – you know what – all the way to Cairo.

The road along north Africa to Cairo is paved all the way. Eventually, we reached the desert – not a sand dune desert – but one that, at least where it approached the coast, was covered by a low shrubby growth. Often, the road stretched straight to the horizon. Sometimes we cut the brush as padding for our tent, as we did not carry air mattresses to save weight. Nevertheless, by trip's end the bottom of my tent resembled a sieve caused by rock punctures. Small stores along the road's about 1,500 miles afforded us to replenish food supplies, also gasoline and water. We quickly took to an air-dried, salt and paprika-covered lean beef, called *pastorma*, to fry up. When, one time, we felt like scrambled eggs with fried *pastorma*, we – joy over joy – came across some kids selling baskets of small eggs beside the road by a village. We bought all of them. At camp that night, after frying some *pastorma*, I cracked the first egg – and half of it plopped into the frying pan. They had all been cooked for preservation!

In many places along the road the earth was covered by reflecting splinters – glass – a remainder of the north African war. And it rained in northern Africa, at least in the fall. There were days when we got soaked in the morning, only to have air-dried again by afternoon.

Camel herds crossing the desert, had to be watched for, since these creatures often stopped short of the road, only to step onto it, just prior to our arrival at that spot, a potentially deadly event. We all had visas for Egypt, and when we entered this country, lying farther south, we enjoyed the warmth we had missed. With no sun screen available at the time, just plain Nivea cream, the skin of our noses came off in sheets.

Eventually, we entered the chaos that was Cairo and somehow learned of a lodging place for foreigners, run by German Lutheran Sisters! We found acceptance there and, through the following days explored the city, where we got to know an elderly Jewish couple at a market place – yes, there were still Jews living in Egypt at the time – who invited us for dinner. I felt honored, being German! But we never made it to the Egyptian Museum, since, a few days after our arrival, Britain, France and Israel attacked Egypt because of Nasser's expropriation of the Suez Canal. For at least ten days we were now stuck at our place of residence. It had become too dangerous for us foreigners to venture into the city. We occupied a small room on the roof of the multistory building and from there were able to watch the air raids of the attackers outside the city.

Prior to the attack, new people had arrived at our place, among them a German girl in her early twenties, who appeared quite naive to us even younger, but by several days more experienced travelers. We cautioned her to wash all fruit with potassium-permanganate, the only means available to us to sterilize fresh produce. She proudly told us the next day that she had washed also some sesame seed-covered bread sticks in such a solution. And to top it off, she went out for dinner with a dashing Egyptian army officer, against our warning. A young

German fellow showed up with red pustules all over his body. He had been an overnight guest in a bedouin's tent and had become the victim of bed bugs. Two, a bit older German globe trotters claimed to have been the models for a German author's trilogy of former P.O.Ws, who, escaped, traveled the world. I had read the three books and, from what I recalled, their exploits sounded true.

The food at our lodging place consisted in a large part of rice, of which we quickly grew tired, longing for fried potatoes that were served only once a week. One day I splurged to sneak to a German restaurant, where I delighted in a square meal of sausages with sauerkraut and mashed potatoes. Already in Libya we had grown tired of the Arab flatbread, like pita bread, and were happy when we found small breads Italian-style, Libya having been an Italian colony, where this kind of bread had been introduced. Later, in Cairo, it was interesting to watch delivery boys in the morning, transporting huge trays of this flat bread, which, fresh from the oven hadn't flattened yet, but was round, almost like balloons. We also fixed ourselves between meals a helping of fried *pastorma* with scrambled eggs, and – shame on us – followed local custom and tossed the egg shells off of our rooftop abode, down onto the street. Yes, there was some danger walking the streets. People sitting evenings on their balconies, masticating bits of sugar cane, spit the leached remains onto the street. And thus, woe to the passer by below, who, at times, might also be threatened by a pail of dumped wash water.

I had become friends with an Austrian, 30 years of age, who had lived for years all along the north African states, and spoke fluent Arabic. Of course, with that experience, he was much more worldly than I. When a hefty, 50 year old German woman nurse, bicycling from Germany via Spain, all along the north African coast, to inherit a farm in Kenya – another one, but who knows what this was about – offered to darn my socks, my Austrian friend cautioned me, saying, "Herb, she's after more than your socks!" I followed his advice. One evening, after we were able to hit the streets again, he also introduced me in a social setting to a couple of Egyptian women. One, about 35 of age, was married to a German, who was stuck in Germany, since all air traffic was still suspended due to the war. Her pretty cousin, about my age, had just been divorced from her Egyptian husband. What left an indelible impression on me, was how the two ladies tore into the fabric of their Muslim culture and religion!

Our ventures onto the streets resulted twice in a crowd suddenly gathering around us, shouting, "Anglesi, Francaui," "Englishmen, Frenchmen," thinking we were downed pilots –

of all things! We quickly tried to spot a man with eye glasses in the crowd, likely better off and educated, speaking English, but then were both times taken to a police station for identification. I recall, that on one of these times, the commanding officer, realizing that my companion was Austrian, and knowing that Hitler had been Austrian, was all agush. We had it made. At the time, the Arabs were fond of Germans and Austrians, although, they did prefer East Germans to West Germans. Ah, well, I can't please them all.

With the outbreak of war, foreigners were evacuated on ships upstream the Nile to be flown out of Khartoum in the Sudan. At the time, the Aswan Dam did not exist yet. We hardy souls opted not to be evacuated and stayed put. The disadvantage was, that our meager travel money, Egyptian pounds, quickly dwindled. But, visiting the British Consulate, I was able to convince the official to issue us visas for Kenya, by showing him my 2,000 marks in British pound traveler checks. We had made it to the Pyramids and the Sphinx – the Museum had been closed – but before we set off for Aswan, the German bicycling nurse had returned, peddling 500 miles to Aswan, where the Sudanese immigration officer, never mind that he did not look very officer-like as we, too, found out, had asked her to see him after five P.M. over there-and-there to stamp her visa. She went, only to slap his face – and peddle back

500 miles to Cairo – where we actually met her for the first time, when she complained at the Sudanese consulate.

When the war hubbub had died down, and we were told that banks would honor British pound traveler checks again, we thought it high time to head south. I had "Germans" painted in large, yellow Arabic letters on the the lid of the sidecar, and off we went. We had been warned not to camp just anyplace, but evenings to check in with police stations to inquire there for a camp site. So we did that first evening. An officer asked us to wait until 5 P.M., and when that time came, he invited us to follow him, together with a colleague. We were taken to a former British guest house and the two men treated us to a complete dinner and fed us, a first, pomegranate. Then we were offered beds in one of the rooms, unfortunately, we had to leave the windows open for air and coolness, and I spent the night with only a small air hole to breathe from under my sheet, trying to ward off the mosquitos.

Arab people are very hospitable! We were always received courteously and the first offer was usually for either Turkish coffee, black tea, or – Coke. I took to Turkish coffee with a vengeance and, getting every time a bit too deeply into the suds – was close to having a gastritis upon my return to Germany. The following evening saw us arrive at another police station in the country. We became the 'event of the day' to these men who, far from 'civilization,' along the banks of the Nile, maintained security. Five or six gathered in the yard of the police station and it became a lively evening. Traveling along the Nile, it's vividly green valley bordered on both sides by the beige desert, we observed Archimedes Screws and other man- and donkey-powered water lifting devices for the irrigation of fields. At one time, driving through a small village, the locals minded our passing and pelted us with stones. I gunned up the engine, and we quickly escaped over a levee.

We reached Luxor the following day, and after visiting the Ramseseum, crossed the Nile to view the Colossi of Memnon, and rode a painful trek on donkeys, because of their staccato steps, to the Valley of the Kings. Entering Ramseses and King Tut's grave chambers was very impressive! And, would you believe it – we were the only two tourists there – because the 'regulars' had all been evacuated. On the way back we walked Queen Hatshepsut's Temple, again the sole visitors, and many years later, when I learned of the 50- plus tourists that had been murdered by terrorists on its premises, I recalled the openness of the building and that there was no cover, none at all, to find protection. From a local, who had approached us, I purchased a pharaonic image, chiseled from a wall – or, most likely, a replica.

Now the road was no longer paved. Still following the Nile Valley, it lead into the desert and was now a dirt road washboard. The brackets of the cycle's Plexiglas windscreen broke and the rig had to be dumped. Then Aswan lay ahead. Our cash, our Egyptian pound currency, had been totally depleted by now, and we figured on cashing in a British pound traveler check in the city. Alas, we had been misinformed, and checks were still not accepted. Broke, we were! We drove to the Sudanese immigration office and presented our visas. The 'officer' in his jellaba frock stepped outside, looked at our vehicle, shook his head, and said: "No entry." He didn't even ask for us to meet him after hours at his home. . . Well, many years later I realized that the man had possibly saved my life. My underpowered motorcycle would most likely have given out in the Highlands of Ethiopia, with us being stuck there for transportation, or having to rely from thereon on whatever local contraptions would be available.

But there we stood now, our last hope gone for exchanging checks in the Sudan for cash. We drove back and forth through Aswan – not that there was much to travel through – until we saw the German license plate on a Mercedes car. We tracked its owner down to a dingy room in a 'hotel,' where he lounged with two rather attractive German women, but of unknown persuasion. The trio was also on the

110

way to Kenya, but I do not recall whether they, too, looked to inherit a farm there. When I told him of our calamity, he suggested that he knew of a local merchant, who closed his shop late in the evening, and a little hit on the head might net us some cash. Hearing this, I slowly backed out of the room. And, once more, we cruised Aswan. Then, lo and behold, I spotted the sign of a Protestant Mission, highly unusual in a Muslim country, where it is forbidden trying to convert Muslims. But there live also plenty of Coptic Christians. I drove up to the building and met the missionary, telling him of our predicament. Surely, he had met plenty of run-down characters looking for a handout, but after I showed him my travelers checks, he relented and lent me ten Egyptian pounds. Hurrah, we were liquid again! I left him my lightmeter as security, and once back in Cairo, repaid him through the Sisters of our lodgment. Believe it or not – a year later I received it back. A Sister from the Mission had vacationed in Germany, where she had met my Godmother, also a Sister. And so I got my lightmeter back, which I had written off.

But we did not have enough cash to journey on. There was only a miserable 30 mile long roadway from Aswan, in Egypt, to the Sudanese border, from where we could have picked up a train to carry us to the Ethiopian border, but with the Sudanese immigration man having said "no," this was no longer an option. So we decided to drive back to Cairo, and out of Aswan we went, to pitch our tent in the desert. By 11 P.M., both unable to sleep, we decided "enough." We packed up, and through the night into the following day, drove the about 500 miles back to the Cairo.

It was a bad time! The attack on Egypt was past, but the uprising in Hungary against the Soviets was in full swing. What to do? My relationship with my traveling companion had not been the best. He smoked and had contributed much less to our travel kitty. I felt like giving up and going home. My Austrian buddy was also ready to head for Austria and would join me on the trip back. I was able to obtain a cash advance from a business friend of my father's in Cairo, which enabled me to drive back. Thus, I paid off my companion, who wanted to stay or go on – and I later learned – he made it to Addis Ababa, in Ethiopia – with the 50 year old nurse! He also must've had socks to darn. Having come into money again, I purchased some mementos, a rug, some silver-inlaid copper ware, and other goodies which, later, at home, let me create a traveler's ambiance in my room.

Then it was time to pack, and the Austrian and I drove along the north African coast, but this time westward. At el Alamein we walked the sea of white crosses of fallen German soldiers, where Rommel's dash for the Suez Canal and the Middle Eastern Oil in Iraq had come to a halt. Near Tobruk, we spent the night with two German workmen, who were in the process of re-interring the bones of German soldiers into small fiberglass coffins, which, in turn, were stored in a broad-based, tower-like masonry building. One evening, after we had entered Libya, we came in the midst of nowhere across a stalled British military vehicle with its driver, a red-faced young recruit and a chaplain standing next to it. Their radiator had run dry and they were stuck. We stopped, but since we happened to have a minimal supply of water, just enough for ourselves for the night, we had to leave them to their fate. Our only suggestion was, that they could pee into the radiator, for their car to carry them some distance farther. Camping in the desert along the way, we dined on onions, which we ate like apples, being short of other vegetable matter. But, one evening, we also savored a plentiful

supply of Bismarck Herring, marinated, rolled up filets of herring with a pickle inside, a German delicacy. Wonder over wonder, I had discovered this can in a Cairo store. Camping one night, we heard noises in the distance, causing us to sleep lightly. In the morning, we discovered that a shepherd with his flock of goats and camels had come close to our tent, and soon, came ambling towards us. We were just preparing breakfast, and my Arabic-speaking friend invited him to join us in our repast of scrambled eggs, fried *pastorma*, flatbread, and black tea. It was interesting to observe how the man accepted our invitation, not partaking in the *pastorma*, which could have been pork, and making my friend first taste everything, even the tea, before he partook.

In Benghazi we boarded a ship to Sicily. But before we left, we had been flagged down on the road near Benghazi by some Germans, who, after release by the British from being P.O.Ws, had stayed in their service at the local British air base. They invited us to their own recreational facilities on the base, where I was introduced to plenty of Scotch, neat. It became a miserable night sleeping on matting in their gym! Mind you, it wasn't the matting. On boarding the ship, we noticed a noisy, beer guzzling group of these Germans, bidding one of their own farewell. Talking to him later, it turned out that he had a daughter in my hometown. Meals on board were limited. Next day's lunch was a plate with some boiled potatoes, a bit of salad and − an entire, about 7" long boiled octopus. I didn't touch the critter; my worldly Austrian buddy consumed also mine. A steady oncoming swell got our ship, heading straight into it, to rock, but lying on my bed, caused sea sickness not to become too bad.

And then there was Messina. We crossed the Strait of Messina and began to drive northward. The first evening on the mainland found us in a little vaulted cavern restaurant where we enjoyed a dish of fried freshwater fish. My friend asked the innkeeper whether he could find us a place to sleep. A little while later he asked us to follow out the back door to another house. Upstairs an elderly couple greeted us, after which we slept in their bed they, for the night, on a sofa. It was a most friendly, clean and neat experience.

However, my cycle had had it, and wouldn't pull the two of us up bigger hills. So, my buddy had to walk part of Italy, until I/we decided it was enough and we took a train, cum cycle, to Rome. I had it fixed at a D.K.W. service and off we went to the Italian-Swiss border at Chiasso. It was now the latter part of December and too cold to journey on with our insufficient clothing. Another train was boarded. In our compartment we met an Israeli military officer. When we mentioned to him where we came from, and that we had never seen an Egyptian fighter plane in the skies during the attack, he commented that "Egyptian pilots are excellent flyers and top gunners, but they can't do both together." A trip to the train's diner – there was no need to skimp anymore – introduced me to Gorgonzola cheese, and I never fell out of love with it again. Then, on December 24, my Austrian buddy had left the train somewhere – I arrived in Mainz and drove across the Rhine River to ring the bell at our house in early morning. I believe it was the nicest Christmas present I ever made my mother!

So, I had not accomplished what I had set out for, but . . . A trip like this, even if it was only for barely three months, was something unusual for the time, shortly after W.W.II. I had plenty to talk about and quickly made all kinds of friends. While it then took me 25 years to see Africa again, this time in style, on a Kenyan and Tanzanian safari, my North African stint nevertheless had opened the world for me, never to close again.

A Hike in Provence

A few years ago, my wife and I took a hiking trip through Burgundy and Alsace with Randonnée Tours. Such trips can be booked with any number of friends participating. The tour operator books overnight stays in hotels or B & Bs along the route, with their local rep transporting the luggage from inn to inn so that hikers carry only a day pack.

In 2004, the time had come for us to experience a bit of Van Gogh's Provence. We invited an 80- year-old neighbor friend, a tough-as-nails hiker to join us. From Marseille we took the train up the Rhone valley to Orange near Avignon. A taxi was waiting at the station to take us to our stating point, the ancient town of Vaison la Romaine, not far from Mont Ventoux, highest mountain in Provence.

Vaison, the "Pompeii of France", dates back to Roman times when it had a population of 10,000 vs. today's 6,000. It lay on the Agrippan Way leading from Arles to Lyon. A retirement place for Roman legionnaires, it had a beautifully located theater and all the conveniences a Roman could expect, with two aqueducts to bring in water. Much has been excavated and restored. A little museum has some splendid displays. A Roman bridge still spans the Ouveze River. A medieval village, beautifully maintained and a castle ruin, all on a protective hillside, overlook modern Vaison, once called Vasio Vocontiorum. We walked the steep narrow streets of the old town several times in the two days we had allotted and enjoyed a couple of excellent four-course dinners in its restaurants. My wife could not resist purchasing fabric for a table cloth in the typical colors of Provence.

Our route description challenged us with a 22 km hike for the first day from Vaison to the village of Gigondas. We had agonized whether to do it all, or to cut it in half by taking a taxi to the midpoint as recommended by the tour operator's self-guide instructions. But our gung-ho octogenarian friend Grant   was all for doing the whole thing. So we did – kind of. The local rep had advised us that the first part of the hike was not very interesting – and that turned out to be true. Up and down through forest and brush, into and out of ravines slippery from a night's sprinkle. By midday we had arrived at the hill town of Seguret, by which time my wife Ute had had enough and I needed to beg a not-too-cooperative bistro owner to call a taxi for her - which he did, once I told him it was for my wife - not for me. In ten minutes it arrived and in another ten she was at our destination, the Hotel Les Florets. Grant and I continued the hike on foot, which from there turned out to be very lovely. It took us four hours to complete.

The hotel was located outside Gigondas near the Dentelle Mountains, an uplift range of limestone, clay and salt and, as its name says, looks like a row of teeth. We had two days to recuperate from our exertion. The English-speaking hotel owner provided us with plenty of red Domaine wine and excellent food. Hilariously, when I asked him one evening to suggest the most pungent, potent cheeses from the cheese cart, he said: "I hate cheese", to which I responded: "But that is utterly un-French". Having two days at Les Florets we took a taxi to the nearby hill town of Sablet to look around.

The trails, sometimes narrow foot paths, sometimes forest or agricultural roads, are marked by blazes. The routes mostly follow established long-distance hiking trails. Sometimes, though, some reconstruction has recently occurred or a mistake crept into the route description and the hike became a brief orienteering adventure. From then on, our daily hikes took us through open woodlands, vineyards and fields, along beautiful vistas of an ancient, well-maintained and cultivated landscape, reminding us at times of Tuscany and Umbria. Sometimes the call of a cuckoo followed us. By now we had smartened up and asked our local rep to give us a ride part way when he transported our luggage to the next inn. Some may call it cheating, but we felt to have paid our dues to Provence on the first day's 22 km.

From Les Florets, at Gigondas, the trail now led to the town of Le Barroux and our next hotel, Les Geraniums. We, however, started only at the village of Beaumes-des-Venise, halfway along the trail route. Although we never used the topo map provided, we had been wise to avoid some of the steeper hillsides here. Le Barroux turned out to be another pretty hill town, fun to walk, with an old castle on top of the hill. Our tour description told, that it had been sacked by retreating German troops in 1949. We were amazed that my fellow-Germans were supposed to have held out that long in Le Barroux. Pity they had to wreck it, though. Sitting on the hotel terrace with a view across a valley, we enjoyed a bottle of red wine, which friend

Grant had to pay for because of a bet he'd lost. Then we had another delicious four-course meal at Les Geraniums. It has been my experience, that, despite all the walking, I generally gain about 4 lb on every such trip, whether it be in France or Italy. I therefore caution the reader to seriously consider this side effect before rushing into such a booking.

Next we were off to the B & B, La Demeure du Manon in Malaucene. This time we didn't "cheat", but hiked the 11 km without the aid of transportation. This section of the hike led through a more open countryside of fields and always, always vineyards. And, in this early May, the scent of the famous "Herbs de Provence" accompanied us on most stretches of our hikes, whether through woods or fields. At some point, when taking our snack lunch at a field's edge, a couple came by. They turned out to be Dutch vacationers who often spend their annual holiday in this same location. We had an enjoyable talk with them. An enclosure we passed along the trail had a sign posted that truffles were protected here. Upturned soil in various locations told us of the presence of wild boar and the need for the enclosure.

The final leg of the day's trip led over a range of hills through scrub oak forest. At many locations, the trail was bordered on the upslope by an ancient wall as if it had once been an old roadway connecting settlements. Then, suddenly, I spotted a massive stone structure in the woods, a bit off the trail. It turned out to be a borie, built of massive limestone slabs piled on top of each other, walls and ceiling forming a domed enclosure. Quite roomy, but cold inside, the former occupants must have been very sure of their handiwork to dwell inside such a construct. Later we learned that such bories were built from time immemorial to well into the 19th century at various locations in France as well as other places in the world whenever fields needed to be cleared of stones and timber was scarce.

Off the mountain, we arrived in Malaucene at the mansion of La Demeure du Manon, originally the police station, now beautifully and tastefully converted by Madame Sylvie Blanc to a B & B. The large peaceful garden in back with its sitting areas, pool, fruit trees and frog pond was a delight. Even more so was the hospitality and graciousness of the owner. Fortunately, we had two days here to enjoy the countryside, the hospitality, the nightly frog concert and once again - the good food at a restaurant across the street. Madame Blanc took us on a 15 min ride to Vaison to experience the local market, a sight to behold: everything from cheap and not-so-cheap clothing, garden supplies, flowers, cheeses, meats, fish, and what not was being offered.

And then it was time to leave again. François, our rep, gave us a ride to Le Crestet, this truly a hill town, ancient and most beautiful, with a number of foreign painters depicting the sights from a small plaza at the top, flanked by a castle ruin. The place is so steep, that a passage from one level to the next is chiseled into the rock. Even my slight acrophobia did not deter me from climbing the stairs in the 60° slope. From Le Crestet, a pleasant hike through the woods, where we met an English couple on a similar excursion, took us back along our circular route to Vaison la Romaine.

Next day the taxi dropped us off at the railway station in Orange. There it turned out that the French railroad workers had gone on one of their one day strikes. Stuck! A bus to Marseille? But from where in Orange, dragging our luggage? And would we still catch our flight? Well, there are always taxis! For the small charge of 160 Euros we made it in time for our flight. And in the departure terminal we two men were "treated" to a French farewell. Needing to use the washroom and upon stepping to the urinal, I was greeted by a sudden puff of warm air, causing me to jump back involuntarily. Fortunately, there was no one in the room to laugh. I cautiously approached the device again only to be greeted by another puff. Knowing now that I could not avoid being "puffed", I held my position. I could not help, though, exposing my friend, Grant, to also encounter this unique and inexplicable French experience. But by that time, we already had plenty of experience in jumping and walking across the beautiful Provence countryside.

Touring in Germany

While Lufthansa had set us down safely at the Munich airport in May of 2004 returning from our hike in Provence, I literally had to commandeer an off-duty rail employee to extract our tickets from the resistant automatic dispenser for our ride on the rapid transit into town. And never forget to validate your tickets before boarding, just as you must do in France and Italy.

That evening, friends of many decades, living part of the time in Munich, part in Houston, invited us for a sumptuous dinner at their penthouse. With lots of their good advice we explored the sights of the city the next day on a city tour. Of the many good museums in Munich we only visited the Deutsche Museum, which has the most extensive technology exhibit in Europe, and in some respects may rival the Smithsonian. Our friends' recommendation to visit the Haxenbauer restaurant, right next to the Hofbräu Haus, for Kalbshaxe and Schweinshaxe (veal and pigs' knuckles) we consummated the next evening. Their herbed salad was out-of-this-world.

The following morning we picked up a BMW 318 for our excursion. Once we had found our way out of the city, I gave the car a spin on the Autobahn, taking it up to 160 km/h (100 miles/h), which made our friend Grant who was traveling with me and my wife a bit uneasy. Then we picked up the Romantic Road, taking us north toward Rothenburg ob der Tauber. Through rolling hills and beautiful varicolored fields, many in bright-yellow canola (rape) patches, we stopped at the ancient town of Nördlingen, which lies inside the 15 million year old 25 km diameter Ries Crater. Up and up we climbed the unending-appearing stairs of the 90 m high church bell tower to survey the distant eroded crater walls Apollo 14 & 17 astronauts visited.

Then Rothenburg beckoned. Yet when we arrived there the gates to the ring-walled medieval town were closed. No siege had been led, no, it was to provide peace in town for pedestrians and the many open-air restaurants. A walk-in and inquiry enabled us to reach the Markus Turm Inn after all, outside old, inside with all the modern conveniences. Beautifully located Rothenburg, overlooking the Tauber River, was a Free City in medieval times, rich through the wool trade and well defended, until, in the Thirty Years War it fell to Catholic forces of Emperor Charles the Fifth. Thereafter it lingered, until it was discovered for its picturesque sights at the turn of the 20th century, also by the American McCloys, whose son grew up with a picture of Rothenburg in his home in America.

In 1945 Allied bombing destroyed 40% of the old town since Hitler had decreed it to be defended to the death. Fortunately, sense prevailed. The now assistant Secretary of State, John McCloy remembered and issued orders against further destruction by artillery barrages if it could be avoided. While the German commander was out of town for some consultation, the besieging American commander met with the German colonel in charge and the latter agreed to vacate the town. Hooray!

The postwar monetary contributors for the rebuilding of the town, among which are a number of Americans, could 'purchase' one or multiple meters of the town wall on which they were and are honored by plaque inlays.

On an evening walk through town this story and many other most interesting ones on Rothenburg's history were personably and most colorfully told the mostly American audience in flawless English by a make-believe night watchman in medieval outfit and halberd. During the tour he pointed out the oldest house in Rothenburg, nowadays housing a Weinstube (wine restaurant). Its name was 'The Hell'. At the end of our walk he playfully suggested "and now you can go to Hell".

The following morning we departed for the hamlet of Detwang, just outside Rothenburg. Settled in 960 it features a small Romanesque church begun in 968 with a Tilman Riemenschneider altar. In the early 1500s Riemenschneider carved a number of highly elaborate wooden altars, several meters high and wide, which were hinged and could be folded up for safe storage in case of war. Continuing through pleasant valleys and over hillsides, we crisscrossed the land on always excellent small country roads, stopping also at the Herrgotskirche in Creglingen with another Riemenschneider.

In the afternoon we arrived at the village of Jagsthausen, where at age eight, I had spent a year at the end of The War, yet had retained many fond memories of its surroundings. I had made reservations to spend a night at the castle of the Götz von Berlichingen. In 1945 the youngest Götz, or Count, was more or less like one of the village boys, a year older than I, and with him we also roamed the castle grounds. Sadly I learned that he had passed away ten years ago.

Goethe memorialized the Götz of the 30 Years War in a play still enacted every year in the castle courtyard. The play's highlight is when the Götz, who had sided with the Protestants and with his castle besieged, was asked to surrender by an outside-waiting emissary of Charles V's army. Reenacted in the play, while standing at a window, he pulls down his trousers and turning, shouts to him "Tell your Colonel, he can kiss my arse". Now you know, where this famous term comes from – at least one version.

It was a pleasure walking the creaking floors of the castle, imagining the gathering of family and nobles of the past, and sleeping in one of the rooms where who-knows had slept already, but all today with modern conveniences. A wonderful dinner of venison, wild boar and pheasant complemented by a few glasses of mellow Würtemberger Red in the castle restaurant completed the evening.

Arriving in Bad Marienberg in the Westerwald Mountains northwest of Wetzlar, we learned that my wife's mother at age 93 had passed away there the day before. That entailed a change in plans. My wife Ute immediately began making funeral arrangements with the help of her siblings and to arrange for her modified return trip to the States. I was between a rock and a hard place, my wife's loss and funeral preparations and our friend Grant's inability to speak a word of German. So, after some consideration I took off with him northward to Bad Lauterberg to consummate some business commitments and from there to the ancient town of Goslar in the Harz Mountains.

Goslar features among its many other medieval sights, such as the Rathaus (the Town Hall), the market place with its beautifully restored old buildings and peculiar inscriptions and figurines, the Kaiserpfalz. This grand building, which has seen good and bad times, was one of several, but the most beloved residence of the German Traveling Emperors of the Holy Roman Empire. They traveled for reasons to keep a check on trouble-making local chieftains and to dispense law. Because of the missing infrastructure, they had to move on to the next imperial residence once the retinue of the Emperor, several hundred men and horses, had eaten up the local supplies!

And since the oldest German restaurant, Zum Brusttuch (At the Bib), was closed, we too had to move and enjoyed instead an exotic dish at a Ceylonese restaurant. To work off calories we hiked up the Rammelsberg overlooking Goslar. Beneath it lay the reason for Goslar's fortunes, silver mines, now spent. A mining museum and mine tour are today's attraction. Another evening the Kaiserworth restaurant presented us with a delightful game dish with Crepes Suzette for dessert.

Agonizing about my abandoned wife, I resolved to leave friend Grant to fend for a day for himself, but provided him with addresses of English-speaking friends in case something should happen to me. Then the Autobahn took me 300 km on a fast drive back for the funeral and to drop off my wife the next morning at the Frankfurt airport. By noon I was back in Goslar where Grant had had a McDonald's hamburger the previous evening for supper and had checked on a rail trip back to Frankfurt, just in case I would have abandoned him.

Farther north we drove toward Jever near the North Sea coast with a brief stop along the way visiting the widow of a long-dead business friend. She would have loved to move to Zimbabwe, alas, Mugabe and his cronies had made it impossible. In Jever we were met by a dear friend of many years, who showed us the dikes and sights of this, his home in northern Germany, today the country with the most windmills in the world. Although Germans are very "green", many have become disgusted with what they call in a literal translation "the asparagusation" of the land. Searching for a restaurant offering Dover sole, we finally found one – with three small filets of sole on my plate, making me feel like I was eating babies, which they were. Gone were the large filets of decades past when I visited there on business. This was overfishing experienced!

A six hour drive took us south to Biebrich, my hometown of the early years, a suburb of Wiesbaden. Our house is or was just about sixty meters off the Rhine River and we stayed in a hotel next door. On our last day we booked a trip down the Rhine to the town of Bacharach of Burt's fame. On board our steamer we were joined by a young American who was herding a group of ten teenagers through parts of Germany for a computer technology competition. His charges were from assorted countries, one from Egypt, two from Japan, one from Turkey, several from the States, etc. He, married, lived in Saudi Arabia. That's Globalization at its best!

On a day trip through the Taunus mountains we visited the Saalburg, a restored Roman fort northwest of Frankfurt. It was one of several spaced along the Limes Wall extending from

Düsseldorf on the Rhine all across Germany to Regensburg on the Danube. The Limes was completed after the Romans had lost three Legions in an invasion of northern Germany, wiped out to the last man by Germanic tribes. Modern Germans are proud of this accomplishment, yet, who knows, had the Romans settled and civilized the entirety of Germany, maybe, just maybe, my countrymen would have been less trouble in later years. The excellent museum of Roman artifacts displays a wide variety of ancient tools of various trades. Two bulbous glass bottles, about 6" tall with narrow necks, had a little handle attached on one side with a small spout at a 90° angle from it. Roman baby bottles!

One of the evenings we had dinner at an adjacent Mexican restaurant serving delicious Mexican-American food. I have known it for at least 20 years. Started by an American for US troops, it also became popular with Germans. Today it is no longer in US hands. The waitress was Greek, her boyfriend and owner looked Indian. That too is Globalization at its best!

At our final breakfast at the hotel, chatting with the new hotel owner, I told him that I had lived next door for many years and that the Rhine at times spills its banks, with two feet of water inundating the ground floor and basement not uncommon. I think I made his day. Then our day had come too to return to Frankfurt for the flight home.

From the Namib to the Okavango and Beyond.

Part 1, Namibia

June 5 to 16, 2005

The Namib desert, with 80 million years the oldest desert on the planet, stretches along the southwest African coast, and has given the country, Namibia, its name.

Why Africa? What is its allure to me to travel to this continent for the fifth time. For my wife, Ute, the third. For almost the entire month of June 2005 we took a safari, meaning a 'long journey', through four countries, Namibia, Botswana, touching on Zambia, ending our trip in Cape Town, South Africa. It wasn't what is customarily thought as being a safari. Sure, we saw plenty of wildlife, but we met many good and interesting people, experienced often stark but beautiful lands, and enjoyed practically everywhere the comforts of civilization.

It all began some time around 1946 when I began to read. My country, Germany, lay in ashes and reading material dated from before Nazi times, often going back to the turn of the century - 1900. Readings, of the by then long gone German colonial period, told of exciting adventures to a boy of ten. Much later did I learn that little was rosy about this period. But I did come across stories playing in German Southwest Africa, as Namibia was then called. In later years it was the wildlife that fascinated me. When I acquired a degree in anthropology my interest in our origins in the Dark Continent was added.

My first attempt to see some of this continent took place in 1956 when, at age 20, I intended to motorcycle from Germany all the way through East Africa to Cape Town. It ended in Aswan, Egypt, due to the British, French, Israeli attack on Egypt. Then, in the 1980s my wife and I safaried in Kenya and Tanzania. In 1995 we traveled through Zimbabwe. I took a circuit through Morocco in 2000. And finally, after 58 years, I ventured to Namibia, the country that had triggered my interest in Africa.

A flight from Phoenix to Atlanta, then by South African Airways via Ilha del Sal, a refueling stop off the Senegal coast near Dakar, to Johannesburg, plus another 'hop' from Joburg, as it is also called, brought us to Windhoek, the capital of Namibia, located in a huge ancient caldera. That last hop in an Airbus

A319, that had seen only 32 commercial flying hours yet. Our entire safari required 14 flight segments in anything from a big Airbus A340-800 to a four-seater Cessna, the flights across the Atlantic taking a grueling 20 and 22 hours.

Our trip organizer, the African Safari Co. in the state of Washington, had arranged accommodation for us at the 1905-built Heinitzburg Hotel, dating from the German colonial period which ended in 1915 in the course of WW1. Yet everywhere German was still spoken, including by black personnel in the lodges, the guides, and shop owners. We found Windhoek, Swakopmund, Walvis Bay, and much of the rest of Namibia clean and organized. Wherever we came, we drank the water and ate our salads with no detrimental effects.

After an evening introduction, our guide of Wilderness Safaris, Kobus Pienaar, of Huguenot-Afrikaner background, picked us up in a Landrover vehicle the next morning. Our only fellow-traveler was a young, vivacious British woman of Indian background, Leena Lukha, who accompanied us for the first half of our journey until her travel plans led her, to our great regret, in a different direction to the Skeleton Coast in Namibia. So, what would usually have been a group of 6-8 travelers eventually consisted only of our 28 year old, very competent and personable guide, my wife and myself. We had a private safari.

Our first day's drive took us through the Khomas Hochland and the Namib Desert, with a variety of wildlife along the dirt road, such as springbok, oryx antelope, in the Afrikaans language also known as gemsbok, baboons, warthogs, jackals, and others, to the Kulala Tented Camp, an outpost of civilization in a stark mountainous wilderness. The nine permanent safari tents and its lodge were managed by a 22 year old white Namibian woman, a black management trainee, and at least 12 additional helpers. Wilderness Safaris is obligated to train black Namibians in the management of its camps to eventually have many of them run by black Namibians. We were greeted by a most friendly staff, a three-course dinner, good beds, hot shower, as in all camps and, last not least, by a tame meerkat, a recently orphaned foundling near the camp, who loved to be petted on his belly while making the meerkat equivalent sound of purring. There was a small swimming pool we did not make use of, but with a two-night stay we used the opportunity to have some clothes washed and ironed by the lodge staff between morning and evening. We enjoyed our 'sundowner' drive to watch the

125

gorgeous African sunset, due to the dust in the air – there's always dust in Africa – munching on some snacks with a beer or a glass of South African wine, this too a custom practiced at all camps. With the bug-free and dry air we opted to sleep on bedrolls on a raised wooden side roof of our tent to fall asleep under the star-bright southern sky, its profusion of stars reaching to the horizon with the Milky Way and the Greater Magellanic Cloud wheeling overhead. The silence – precious – was absolute, only at times broken by the call of a wild creature.

Then, on our next day's drive was to Sossusvlei, a salt pan close to the coast, where a dry river has been prevented from debauching into the Atlantic Ocean by huge encroaching sand dunes. At Sossusvlei the highest sand dune with 1,000 ft, also one of the world's longest, is Big Daddy. We only climbed an adjoining dune of about one third its height and rather watched more enterprising younger folks make the arduous hour-long climb up Big Daddy, then run down in giant leaps in a fraction of the time it took them to get up.

The vast, sparsely vegetated plain of the Namib is crossed by some deep canyons cut through eons by seasonal rivers. One of them is the Kuiseb. Several months before our departure Prescott friends had given me a book to read, the story of two German geologists, who opted in 1940 to escape into the Namib, or better, this canyon, rather than face years in an internment camp. Written by Henno Martin, one of the men, under the German title translated 'When War breaks out we'll head for the Desert', published under the English title 'The Sheltering Desert', it was a wonderful read. Whenever I mention this book in Namibia my conversation partner had read it too. It seems to be part of Namibian lore, almost a secular bible. For two and one half years the two lived in the Kuiseb essentially by hunting. They had plenty of time to philosophize, their conclusions being still wonderfully contemporary.

The Namib is populated here and there by herds of springbok and other wildlife. Granite boulders and larger inselbergs rise from it. Near one of these outcrops we stopped to walk to thousands of years old Bushman pictographs at what was once a rock shelter for these ancient people. Lunch time found us at a huge granite inselberg. While Ute and I looked for a convenient place to sit down, we found a metal plaque listing the names of a German-Namibian couple, their dates of birth and death. Beside it stood two vases with long-wilted flowers and between them, in a depression guarded by rocks, lay the gray ashes of the deceased. From where they lay one could almost see forever! What a place for the last rest.

Our day ended at the Aonin Dune Camp located on a side of the broad treed wash of the Kuiseb. Upon arrival the camp manager, Hans, and our guide took us a bit into the dune field which stretches for miles along the Namibian coast. A little table was set up and sundowner snacks were 'washed down' with a gin tonic.

On our day's drive we had crossed the Tropic of Capricorn, the southern equivalent of the northern Tropic of Cancer, which crosses through southern Algeria, Libya, and Egypt. When we talk of safaris in Africa, we all too often visualize a tropical, or at least a very warm climate. But we traveled in June, the winter of the southern hemisphere, when the rainy season lasting from November to March is over. And while deserts can get quite warm during the day, their nights are very cold. In many camps we found hot water bottles in our beds! One camp in Botswana measured 39° F one morning, not far from freezing.

At Aonin sitting around the camp fire in the evening, we were joined by Rudolf Dausab, speaker for the local !Khuiseb-Topnaar people who, about 300 strong, live as pastoralists and herders in the lower Kuiseb valley. A very educated man with internet connection and digital camera, having coauthored a book on the native !nara fruit, he lived in the nearby town of Walvis Bay since, where his people live no modern conveniences were available. His grandfather had been a member of the German Schutztruppe of colonial times, who had stayed on and had married a native woman. Next day he took us to an elder of his tribe, Ouma Lydia, a woman who has lost a good part of her eyesight. One of the two eyeglasses I had brought along helped her somewhat, but there is a need for an ophthalmic team to come to these people to check the individuals, even to operate where cataracts are involved.

Before we could visit Ouma (Afrikaans for grandmother) Lydia Swartbooi at a decent time, Kobus Pienaar, our guide, Rudolf, Leena, our British fellow-traveler, and my wife and I took a 'joyride' through the adjacent dunes, viewed some fossilized elephant footprints retained in the ancient river mud, now mostly covered there by the encroaching sand. We learned that the ! nara *Acanthosicyos horridus,* a leafless, thorny, melon-bearing bush of the Namib is an important component of the dune ecosystem and foodstuff for the Topnaar. Its roots reach deep into the ground, while the upper growth offers shelter to desert creatures, but also causes the sand to be caught and to pile up around the ever-growing bush, eventually forming mini-dunes. By the way: The exclamation mark you find ahead of the !nara and !Khuisep-Topnaar signifies a click sound in the Nama language.

Then we got stuck in the sand, had to deflate the Landrover's tires for increased traction, and dig ourselves out.

By late morning we headed for Walvis Bay, the major harbor of the country, just south of Swakopmund, the second-largest Namibian town after Windhoek, the capital. Both Swakopmund and Walvis Bay get their freshwater since colonial times via a pumping and pipeline system from underground flows of the Kuiseb river. But water levels are going down, like everywhere in the world. We headed for the harbor where a small motorboat was waiting for us. Together with about another 12 tourists we proceeded on a harbor cruise, even beyond its confines where Russian and Chinese fishing boats lay at anchor to save the harbor fees.

A substantial wooden framework built by a German businessman a hundred years ago during colonial times still serves as a roosting place for seabirds and for its original intention, to collect their guano. Our cruise boat, past the steering cabin open in the back, provided a padded bench, about 6x10" for us to sit. Then, at three locations in and outside the harbor, after a railing section in the stern had been removed, our captain called names across the waters, waving small fishes. And three times wild, but habituated Cape Fur Seal bulls launched themselves on board onto the by us vacated central bench, we surrounding them. They took their treats amicably, posed with those of us daring a hug for pictures – my wife included – then took off again when asked – with a little help from an offered fish. It was like meeting another species close-up! Ute and I are not afraid of animals, but we known where and when do be cautious. I've learned of a woman who freaked out when the seals came on board. White pelicans swooped by to pick up fish on the wing, Ute being able to touch their wings. Dolphins and other seals cavorted in the waters.

Subsequently the four of us were dropped off at the outer perimeter of the port, a huge sand spit, almost a peninsula, where we were greeted by a burly German-Namibian with his Landrover. A small table with tablecloth and five chairs were set up beside the vehicle, delicious lunch snacks came out of a cooler, and cold sparkling wine completed the repast. Thereafter we took off southward along the coast, on one side the cold Atlantic Benguela current, on the other the towering beige sand dunes. On the return trip our host drove across and through the dune field – the perennial wind erases tracks within hours or days. Never having experienced this, it sure was an exhilarating joyride, particularly when our experienced driver took us several times down the 38° slipface of dunes. When, at one time – I was just ready to call out to Neals to beware of going down backwards, it had been his intention all along – and down we went the steep decline. For one more night we returned to the Aonin Dune Camp.

A short drive up the coast brought us to Swakopmund. Before our trip, I had come across the meaning of the town's name and was now able to delight a number of locals with its definition. Mund is German for mouth, and the Swakop is the dry river debauching there into the ocean. But no one knew the meaning of Swakop. Well, here goes. When the Swakop runs after heavy inland rainfalls its waters turn a deep brown, particularly where it mixes with the clear ocean waters. Swakop is a Nama language word and means: Looks like poop!

Everything is very clean and organized in Namibia and Swakopmund is no exception. Its many buildings dating back to colonial times give it a European feeling. Our accommodation at the Hansa hotel was, just as the Heinitzburg, a venue that could have passed muster in any European or American city. We did some shopping of potato-print fabrics in town and right away shipped them home via FedEx due to our luggage weight restrictions, in Botswana only 26 lbs.

The morning saw us headed north along the coast enveloped in its usual morning fog. It is a barren, lifeless landscape, the southern extent of the long, treacherous Skeleton Coast where many shipwrecks took place, thus the name, resulting from the beached remains of ships – not that we saw any. People stranded here in the past invariably perished; during WW2 a large group could be rescued only with extreme effort. Nowadays, a good road stretches about 160 miles northward, a dirt road another 100 miles. Then still nothing. After approximately 100 miles on a 'salt road', unique in its construction, we turned inland. A 'salt road' is built by grading a dirt road, which needs to be done anyway. Then an about two inch layer of gypsum is applied to it, followed by a spraying with saltwater, then rolled and compacted. And since it rarely rains in coastal areas such a road requires resurfacing only every 2-3 years. Its surface almost rivals that of an asphalt highway.

Turning inland into a stony desert with low mountain ranges we saw the ancient welwitchia plants, thriving in a land so devoid of resources. Eventually, we entered a wildly cut canyonland, occasionally opening a little, occasionally showing some sparse growth of trees, bushes, even grass, were rare floods or underground reservoirs permit their growth. And yet – we saw the dung of desert elephants and black rhino populating this sere land. Then – in the midst of nowhere – there was a rhino research station! Our guide, Kobus, followed the often diverging road tracks as if provided with a homing device, and lo – there, eventually, lay Damaraland Camp. The friendly camp staff of Damara people greeted us, as everywhere in Wilderness Safari camps, with moist, cold towels. Their boss, the tallest, biggest, but not fat, black woman I've ever seen, Lena by name, had the day off. When, at dinner she, at times, leaned back in her chair to let out an uproarious laughter about some joke, she was the expression of human spirit per se. When I hugged her probably 250 lbs at our farewell, I could barely get my arms around her. At these dinners I also heard for the first time the click language spoken by a variety of different tribes, among which are the Bushmen, the Damara, and the Nama. Some of the languages have only one click sound, others have several. Our dinner menu was announced by two speakers, one telling us the menu in English, the other in Damara.

The next day Kobus was able to get us to see the elusive desert elephants from a distance. The terrain we had to cross resulted in a tire change, and since the beasts were up on a mountain slope, it would have been unwise to approach them from below. It's easier for elephants to express any 'displeasure' when they are above you, than when approached from above.

Maybe, I should tell here about the food and drink deprivations we suffered, also the 'daily' routine of game drives. Wake-up time was around 6 AM with porridge, muffins and coffee available by a fire. Then, by 7 AM two to six people took off in an open, canopied Landrover for a drive through the surrounding area in search of game. Sometimes it was futile, more often we saw everything from oryx, kudu, springbok, impala, warthog, baboons, jackals, serval cats, lions, chetahs, once even white rhino (who aren't 'white', but are distinguished from the black rhino by their 'wide' muzzles. Why, the heck, weren't they called 'wide' rhinos?) and assorted smaller creatures, particularly often birds like the lilac-breasted roller. At one time I even saw in the high grass three spots of a leopard before it vanished – the Shadow in the Grass.

About two hours into the drive our tracker-guides usually found a secure area for us, their ignorant charges – hey, there are lions out there – and a pit stop for discharge of the morning coffee. Hot coffee, tea, water, or soft drinks were served from the tailgate of the vehicle with assorted snacks. By 10:30 AM we were back at camp for a buffet breakfast with anything from eggs, bacon, sausage, poached tomato, mushrooms, jams, toast, muffins – the works. Buffet-style lunch came at 3 PM. By 3:30 PM the next game drive was on, lasting until about 6-6:30 PM. Well, this game drive too was usually interrupted at a safe area by a sundowner with snacks, beer, wine whisky, gin tonics, etc. at the back of the vehicle, watching the gibbous red-orange sun sink through distant trees below the horizon, cameras happily clicking away.

By 7 PM dinner was served, consisting of various meats, veggies, potatoes, rice, couscous, etc., with wines and beer to accompany them. I might tell here that Afrikaners do live without what we consider vegetables. With only beef counting as meat, as our guide Kobus claimed, all other flesh is considered 'vegetable'!

Under such food deprivation, I'm ashamed to report, I gained six pounds in just under four weeks! Ah – discipline – or its lack!

And something else needs to be mentioned here. In Namibia we traveled with Wilderness Safaris. In Botswana with Kwando Safaris. Wilderness was spiffier!

A long drive from Damaraland Camp took us to the Bushmen's equivalent of the Cro-Magnon cave paintings at Lascaux and Chauvet in France, and Altamira in Spain. There, in the wilderness, in a huge sandstone auditorium flat sandstone slabs are profusely covered with thousands of years old petroglyps of the animals hunted and revered by Bushmen. And yet, I must also convey something else, something told by our guide, whose grandfather operated a cattle ranch in Namibia towards the Botswana border. While our 28 year old guide and his brother, when they were between 6 to 10 year old, were taken for days by a Bushman employee of the ranch into the wilderness to live off it, his grandfather had also held a permit dating to 1905, giving him permission to shoot any Bushman on his land. Bushmen, at the time, were considered non-human. Haven't we come a long way, baby, from the 'good, old times'! Only much later in his life did our confidante learn to appreciate his unique youth-time exposure to bushman lore.

At Damaraland Camp Leena Lukha, to our great regret, went her own way flying out to a camp at the Skeleton coast. In her place arrived three American couples, the men 'hifalutin' businessmen and attorneys from Chicago. With one of them I had a decent chat in the afternoon and it turned out that he knew an old-time friend of ours from Canada as an employee of his. Small world again. That evening, another one joined us at the fire. Somewhat intoxicated from the free wine, he launched into a tirade on the benefits of the 'American way' and in no uncertain terms suggested that all these underdeveloped people ought to follow it. He may have been right in principle, but his presentation was such, that he represented the proverbial 'ugly American'. Disgusted, Ute got up and left. I followed her after a short diplomatic pause.

The next day took us to Ongava Tented Camp in a large private concession southwest of the Etosha Pan. Here we were greeted by Wendy and Cameron, the manager couple, who did their best to make us feel at home. It was here for the first time on this trip, that we were not allowed to walk from our tents to the lodge after dark. Facing the lodge was a water hole, where numerous animals came to drink. But at night also lions and hyenas crossed the camp ground!

One evening, sitting by the fire, glancing up, I saw a fireball blazing with colors, its low trajectory carrying it to its fiery end way beyond the tree line.

Our afternoon game drive had his pleasant sundowner interruption in the presence of three white Rhinos. The return drive in the dark, with Kobus shining his search light into the bushes while simultaneously driving the vehicle, was ugly cold. In the morning we took off for Etosha – the place I first heard about in Africa. The totally flat Etosha Salt Pan extends for 100 by 80 miles in northern Namibia with plenty of all kinds of animals outside the pan. The entry gate to the park and some of the buildings date to the colonial period with its typical castle-like building style. Nowadays, a great number of accommodations have been set up for the many tourists flocking here. A large water hole on one side draws a plenitude of creatures from the largest to the smallest, allowing tourists to gaze at them and take pictures from behind the raised safety of a four foot wall, on its opposite side faced by a six foot wide iron grating to prevent carnivores from jumping the wall.

Upon our return to Ongava other guests and trainees had arrived. One was an exquisitely fine-featured, beautiful young woman, fashionably dressed, a classy lady in demeanor and bearing. Later, I told both my wife and Kobus that, had I been single, I would have liked to invite her for dinner. Kobus said: Oh, you mean the black lady? That she was, light brown, and Kobus said she spoke one of the click languages. It had 'clicked' with me.

And then it was off to Okonjima, a guest farm about 150 miles south of Etosha – we are now on our way back to Windhoek. Okonjima is the home of the Africat Foundation, an organization striving to rehabilitate chetahs and leopards that have been injured, to then relocate them to either reserves or place them on farms, whose owners will not shoot them on sight. It needs to be said here, that most of Namibia is farmland, actually ranch land, except for several large nature parks. Most of the fruit and vegetables consumed in the country are imported from South Africa. Where rehabilitation of the carnivores is no longer possible, they are given the opportunity to live out their lives in a large fenced area. We were taken out to the latter where nine chetahs were called, then fed meat tossed from our Landrover. Even knowing, that these beings had peace and security, it was a sad spectacle! The leopards and chetahs, who know how to hunt, live in a much larger enclosure, and are all equipped with radio collars, by which we were able to track them down.

Guest quarters here are rather fancy permanent structures with thatched roofs, the outside walls open on one side, to be closed by canvas blinds for the night. Sitting there one afternoon reading I watched the birds at the feeding and watering station right outside, birdfood courtesy of our hosts. Within an hour I must have observed ten species of birds, some of beautiful blue and green color. Once, I saw in the distance a couple of eagles gripping talons to cartwheel from the sky.

One evening a group of about 12 guests were driven to a large hide. One of our guides dumped the day's food wastes about 20 feet away from it and soon several honey badgers and porcupines came ambling from the bushes to devour the provisions. It was interesting how the two species got along, feeding often side-by-side. Yet, at times, a porcupine leaned a bit sideways, pointing its enormous spines toward the badger to give it room.

Our best experience, departing one morning on a walk from this fancy lodge, was the Bushman Walk, where a guide, who had lived with Bushmen and a tracker introduced us to Bushman lore. One such introduction was a very simple bird trap, a young woman of our troop dared to trigger. On the second try her hand (the bird) was caught. Then the tracker demonstrated the making of rope from the sansivera plant stalk, by first stripping the plant flesh with a stick from its long internal fibers. He then rolled and wove on his thigh a small 1/8" thick 2-1/2 ft long string from the fibers in the course of only about five minutes – an impressing feat, since Bushmen never require strings exceeding a couple of yards. All you need is the plant stalk, the knowledge and, last not least, a hairless thigh!

Good blacktop roads took us back to Windhoek, having traveled about 1,800 road miles through the country. In Windhoek we traversed half the town to find an Internet Cafe for Ute to send a message to people at home. Never having done it, and us Mac people having to use a cumbersome PC, was a chore. We stayed again at the Heinitzburg Hotel and, for a farewell dinner, we invited Kobus and his lady friend, Sharrol, to an excellent dinner at their restaurant, where Ute and I had the best, most tender springbok filet you can think of. The look from the heights of the Heinitzburg, overlooking Windhoek, is a most pleasant sight. Too bad, our next day's schedule required us to leave it for Botswana.

From the Namib to the Okavango and Beyond

Part 2, Botswana

June 17 to 24

The Okavango river, originating 800 miles to the north in the Angolan Highlands, crosses the Caprivi Strip, a narrow Namibian land extension hugging northern Botswana, giving Namibia access to the Zambezi River. The river then enters Botswana to terminate in a huge inland delta of about 6,000 square miles, sometimes called "The river which never finds the sea". A World Heritage Site, it is one of the most attractive wildlife areas in all of Africa.

To get there, an Air Namibia 12-seater Commander in a two and one half hour flight took us from Windhoek to Maun at the southeastern terminus of the Okavango Delta. Going through Botswana immigration was easy. Visas are non required for US nor German citizens. As everywhere we went on our safari a pickup person greeted us with a sign when we exited from immigration. Stuart was the pilot of the four-seater Cessna that delivered us in a 25 minute hop at only 1000 ft altitude to our next destination, the Kwara Lodge & Tented Camp. From this low altitude we could see elephants and giraffes. Stuart told us, that he had trained pilots in Frankfurt flying 747s; now he worked as a bush pilot flying four-seaters. He thought it more fun. I, too, certainly prefer and enjoy flying low in these small aircraft. If it's a bit bouncier, so what, it can be worse in a big one.

An airstrip appeared in the midst of the savanna, which was speckled with tree islands and individual trees and bushes. Stuart taxied towards the shade of some trees – the "terminal" – where a Toyota safari vehicle stood with our guide-to-be, Jacob, and his tracker, Hub, ready to bring us to Kwara Lodge and Tented Camp. The 650 square mile private Kwara Concession is located at the northeastern fringe of the Okavango Delta bordering the Moremi Reserve.

The camp lies adjacent to a large lagoon, part of the Okavango system, this lagoon now drying up in the rainless winter season. From the lodge, built into and around a couple of huge African Ebony trees, steps led down to a sitting area around a fire place. Through a few more trees one could look out

135

to the lagoon, about 700 feet distant. It accommodated four resident hippos, who surfaced from time to time to bellow their grunts and status across the countryside. During the day a large herd of about 30 impala antelopes moved about the lagoon's perimeter, white pelicans and other birds flew in and out, jackals wandered by, and other creatures paid their visits to drink.

Our tent was the most distant from the lodge, and like at other camps located in wilderness areas inhabited by carnivores, we were required to get to and from our tents only 'under guard' by our assigned guide. And yes, here too, lions cruised the camp grounds during the nights we were there. The second night of our stay, when Jacob escorted us back to our tent, he took a trail meandering along the perimeter of the grove and there, reflecting the shine of our flashlights, or torches, as they called it like good Brits down there, were facing us about twenty pairs of eyes, not too far from our tent. We stopped. A couple of hours before we had seen about twenty sleeping lions not that far from camp. Well? But then Jacob said: "It's the impalas". Saved again.

But back to our arrival. While I looked around the lodge, Ute had gone down the stairs to sit with a lone gentlemen. They were happily chatting away when I finally joined them. We introduced. His name is Gary K. Clarke, former director of the Kansas City zoo for 32 years. Years ago he had escorted a group of tourists on a safari to East Africa and fell in love with safariing and Africa. He quit his job and started his own safari company, Cowabunga Safaris. He was at Kwara leading his 150th safari so far and was booked already for his 200rds in 2010! A congenial, knowledgeable, and cosmopolitan American, he was a joy to talk with during our stay at Kwara. He also had a good sense of humor, every day wearing a different T-shirt with some slogan. When Ute asked him what Cowabunga, the name of his company on his shirt meant, he said: "I was afraid you'd never ask". He said: "It doesn't really have any meaning, it's a made-up word, but..." then handed us his business card, which said: "COWABUNGA – An ancient tradition from the origins of life in the heart of Africa that has since proliferated into an accepted custom in every culture on the face of the globe". Asking Ute to turn it over, it showed two rhinos copulating.

During a later conversation with him, sensing a kindred spirit, I mentioned repeated 'impressions' of mine when overlooking the African savanna landscape with its tree islands.

136

Despite it being so very different from lands I have grown up in or lived, I've always felt a sense of 'being at home' in this African landscape. Gary quickly quoted Richard Leakey as having called this 'Racial Memory'. So – others have felt the same! Yet I have to ask myself: Is my intellect playing tricks? Is it my anthropological interest and training? Or do I truly feel 'at home'?

Years ago, in the mid-eigthies, when we stood at the rim of Olduvai Gorge in Tanzania, a small Tanzanian in a threadbare suit, who had worked for years with the Leakeys, gave us a lecture on human evolution and Olduvai's importance, his talk of a quality equivalent of one given at a Western university. Upon his conclusion and to recognize his competence, I told him, reflecting my knowledge and sentiment: "In the final consequence, we are all Africans!"

No wonder.

At most camps on our trip, just as other tourists did, we stayed usually for three nights, rarely one. The former gave us two full days of game viewing plus, usually, an afternoon drive on the day of arrival and a morning drive on the day of departure. This was certainly enough time at each location to get to see whatever animals populated this area where, aside from chatting with others and reading, there was little else to do. At the two camps we stayed in Botswana, Kwara and Lebala, we were assigned a guide and tracker, the guide taking responsibility for his charges on game drives, at dinner, and as 'guard'. At the dinner table guides and management personnel joined us tourists, but not the trackers, who seemed to be of a slightly different social niveau.

Kwando Safaris, the concession operator in Botswana, used open Toyotas for game drives. These had three tiers of seats at slightly different levels behind the driver (steering from the right hand side). The Tracker sat on a small seat attached to the left front of the vehicle to be able to look down to spot tracks in the sand of the road tracks and the adjoining grass. But both, tracker and guide, from time to time stopped the vehicle and got out to investigate tracks and determine the direction the animal had taken. The guide also stayed in touch by radio with one or two other game vehicles cruising about in different areas, and when one had spotted something interesting, the others also headed for that spot. If the spotted creatures were carnivores, the tracker abandoned his exposed perch at the left front and retired to the safety of the shotgun seat.

137

The dirt tracks, one cannot call them roads at Kwara, are rather rutted, worn, and sandy. Sometimes chasing across them caused, what Ute called 'Shake n Bake', actually more shake than bake. At least our seats were well padded. Our first game drive in the afternoon of our arrival took us through or past several small elephant herds, where some cows expressed their displeasure of our disturbance with trumpeting and brief mock charges. I truly 'enjoyed' the elephants expressing their being upset in this way. Our driver-guides always had the greatest respect for these huge creatures. As we learned later, the reason for the elephants being cagey was, that in past years poaching for ivory had been rampant until the government deployed 900 army troops as anti-poaching units in this remote area. Elephants remember having been harassed and herd members killed in the past so, still today, years after poaching has come to an end, they react defensively.

Then we got word that a leopard had been sighted, and off we went. Arriving at the area, another vehicle guide pointed to where the animal was in the high grasses. We saw them move – the grasses. I even got to see three spots, as I called it – The Shadow in the Grass. A bit later three cheetahs were spotted. Cheetahs like to hang out on small yard-high elevation, maybe former termite mounds, to survey the land for prey. After a while they put on a move when they spotted a lone impala. It was interesting to observe their hunting tactics, how they split up, who took which role, who was ready for the chase. When it was finally time to pounce, the hunter missed by a few leaps. Years ago, in Zimbabwe, we had seen a lion pride take a zebra. This miss – at least for us – was just as well.

On subsequent game drives we got to see, aside from the ever present impalas, giraffes, wildebeest, also called gnu, tsessebe and lechwe antelopes, the latter preferring swamps, hyenas, zebras, and more. We also saw a profusion of earth mounds produced by blind mole rats. On both afternoon-into-the-night drives we found sleeping lions, lots of them, once we counted twenty, all females. This latter group was harassed by a lone hyena. Lions and hyenas are mortal enemies. Finally, with our search lights illuminating the scene, one of the lionesses got up and chased the hyena a distance away. Following this, the hyena began to sound its awful cackle, laughter, and moans to call more of her kind, as our guide told us. And sure enough, there were soon answers in the distance. This caused our sleepy

138

lions to all get up and wander away a bit, only to drop off to sleep again. On another night drive near the lagoon, across from our camp, we watched four lionesses on the prowl, the four lagoon hippos grazing, and hyenas hanging about.

One afternoon, a short car ride took us to one of the many water channels of the Okavango where Jacob and Hub took us on a mokoro ride, this being a dugout canoe poled along the water channels. The 'modern' mokoro is actually a plastic imitation. No more cutting down trees and laboriously adzing them out. Still, it was a pleasantly silent ride through the profusely growing grasses, reeds, papyrus, ferns, along palm-fringed islands, open grass lands and mopane woodlands. At one time we saw a small croc slithering into the water. Otherwise, it was an uneventful ride.

The next afternoon took us on a more vigorous motorboat ride through the channels and lagoons in which a stranger could readily get lost. The ride terminated in a large lagoon, the home of about 20 hippos. It is always difficult to count hippos, since in addition to those being nosy and/or having surfaced to breathe, there are always plenty of others submerged. The submerged, the unknown ones, are actually the most critical, since they may surface where one least expects them. The hippo is the most dangerous animal in Africa and the cause of most human casualties. We retreated to the near-shore of an even larger lagoon to take our sundowner aboard and watched the sun's red disk sink below the opposite shore. With the beginning of dusk we rather speedily motored homeward, swerving through the sometimes wider, sometimes narrower channels. Suddenly, our boatman called out: "Turn around". I did, and saw a huge hippo bull with mouth agape, pushing a big bow wave, expressing his disgust at having his peace disturbed. We had already a safe distance to him and then, hippos are by far not as fast as a motorboat.

Our guide, Jacob, of slender stature, but about six foot three tall, told us that one of his parents had been Bushman. That being the case, he was certainly a tall Bushman. He had learned to read and write only around age ten, but told us, that he was presently reading: Men are from Mars, Women are from Venus. So much for Bushmen living in the bush! And aside from his extensive knowledge of the animal and plant world, he could also discourse about plate tectonics and fault lines in Botswana. He was a very sensitive and caring man, always trying to please,

139

whether on a game drive or at the dinner table. From some liaison he had a little daughter, but was intent on marrying another woman. Maybe I should inject here, that most native people, whether in Botswana or Namibia, are Christians of one sort or another and carry Christian names. Yet his wedding plans were complicated by – behold – a bride price of 15,000 pula, he had yet to assemble. The pula, meaning rain, an appropriate term for a currency, I think, is Botswana's currency and converts at about 5 to 1, making the bride price US$ 3,000. While I do not really know, I assume the guides get free room and board, a small salary, and a month off after three months, during which they work seven days a week. Beyond that, they can accumulate funds only from the tips they receive, which are supposed to be about seven dollars per day. I gained the impression that many guests did not follow that rule. I would have loved to 'buy' the guy his bride. But individuals as well as all African societies, for that matter everyone, must accomplish what they wish or need to accomplish largely by their own efforts. And then it was time to leave Kwara, Jacob and Hub driving us to the tree grove 'airport terminal' for our next half hour Cessna flight to the Lebala Tented Camp.

On our flight to Lebala a couple of vultures whizzed past our six-seater Cessna below, but since we flew a bit higher this time no other wildlife could be seen from the air. At the Lebala airstrip we were picked up by our guide-to-be, Spencer, and his tracker Mr. Mo, so-called, because his native name was too difficult to pronounce for Western tongues. On the ride to camp we quickly noticed that the dirt tracks were smoother here than at Kwara – no Shake n Bake or, should I say, less. The lodge was situated between two water channels, the one in back overgrown by bulrushes, the one in front open. From there, the lodge sitting area, as well as the tents, one looked across the channel onto the tree-dotted African plain. The tents' entrance foyer had a reading and writing area, an open-space shower in the back, from where one looked up into the foliage of a giant tree, and a flush toilet, as in all camps. Here, too, we found hot water bottles tucked into our beds in the evening, a most welcome experience for those cold nights.

Lebala Camp is located next to the perennially flowing Kwando River, nearby turning into the Linyanti Swamp, from which it emerges as the Linyanti River which, in turn, feeds into the Chobe River.

At this camp we were taken on two wild goose chases – not for geese, but once for a leopard, the other time for buffalo, both not productive and enjoyable. But then, one night, we tracked a male lion wandering the dirt track in front of us, finally breaking into his intimidating roar! Earlier that evening, dusk was settling, we encountered a small herd of elephants among open trees and bushes. Our driver had approached them cautiously when they wandered away into the bushes. Suddenly, one of them, displeased, charged our vehicle, trumpeting loudly. Our driver turned amazingly fast, put the pedal to the metal and, branches and leaves slashing our ducked heads, we scrambled for safety. Yes, we did look back while all that was going on, but no one got a picture of the event. I then claimed, that any adventure one survives, is a good one.

There was also a French newlywed couple at Lebala, Vincent and Margot. Nice folks. One afternoon, when we got back to camp the camp manageress told them, that their tent had been attacked by an elephant during our game drive and that they should, please, check that everything inside was okay and properly rearranged. They disappeared and our manager told us smilingly that a private dinner had been set up in their tent. We did not see them any more that evening.

And then it was time to leave again. This time a two-engine plane picked us up. On board was a young couple I started a conversation with while we waited on the airstrip before takeoff. Asking where they were from, they said: Hungary. Their English was excellent. It turned out they were to manage the Kwara camp in the near future and had been on an inspection trip. It made me very happy to find here, in the African bush, good English-speaking people from Central Europe, now partaking in the going-ons of the Western World, or should I say, The World!

We landed at Kasane Airport, nothing much to brag about, although it said 'International'. Kasane is located in the northeastern corner of Botswana. We were picked up punctually, as usual. On our drive out of the airport I noticed elephant dung within the confines of the airport. I would dislike very much to have to land there by night.

We were taken to Kubu Lodge, located on a large acreage alongside the Chobe River, there about 600 ft wide. Guests were warned not to swim from the banks. Crocs! Our accommodation was of a little chalet, the beds furnished with mosquito netting. We were now in the subtropical zone. A few vervet monkeys cavorted in the big trees of the property. Out in the fields farmers grew bananas, mangoes and papayas. That first evening the lodge had a barbecue which included beef, pork, chicken and sausage. I felt like, thus opted for, a good-size steak. Ute did too. Well, had I picked two pieces, I could have taken it to a cobbler to have my boots resoled. It was the toughest piece of meat I've ever come across, impossible to masticate. Our next night's dinner was much better.

The first afternoon we were picked up for a game drive into Chobe National Park. This park houses 45,000 elephants, far too many for its size, and thus it turned out to be severely degraded, the trees stripped of their bark by the 'eles' and toppled by them to get to their upper reaches. Vehicles can travel only along the dirt roads and are thus restricted in what can be seen from there. However, driving along the Chobe River lots of elephants had come to drink. Since, due to the parks proximity to populated areas there had been little poaching, the animals were much less afraid of humans and could be approached more closely. When closing in on the first herd, our 22 year old driver-guide, asked us how close we would be comfortable. Ute told him, "You know what's safe. Just go ahead." And he did, to the effect, that a big bull passed our vehicle at a 10 foot distance, giving us a cautious eye on the way.

The next morning we choose a water craft trip down and along the banks of the Chobe to its confluence with the Zambezi, where four countries have a common border, Botswana, Namibia, Zambia, and Zimbabwe. We followed the antics of a kingfisher, saw several small crocs and monitor lizards, one of them with the respectable length of over three feet.   That evening a larger craft took us upstream together with a French couple for more buffalo, hippo, and elephant sightings, also a rather lazy, but very substantial crocodile.

Now, here's a note of a small unpleasantness, needing to be mentioned nevertheless. Having come to the end of safariing, Ute and I reorganized our backpack and duffle bags. On leaving Windhoek I had received a VAT refund of 300 South African Rand at the airport, about US$ 50.00, which I stuck into some envelope in one of my bags, not giving it much thought during our ongoing trip, and thinking: I'll find it, when we get to South Africa. Note here, that all our cash was divided five times (we don't carry traveler checks) and securely kept. Well, when going through the six compartments, only three being lockable, I was unable to find the Rand currency. Ute, looking through her things, could not find a spare pack of AA batteries. Odd! It could only have happened in Kwara or Lebala, and only while our packs were in our tents.

And then we were to be picked up at Kubu Lodge by a bus of Wilderness Safaris, the good and widely placed company we had traveled with in Namibia, to be taken to the two mile distant ferry to cross the Zambezi. But no one showed up. It got later and later, us not knowing how long it would take to get through Botswana emigration, by ferry across the Zambezi, through Zambian Immigration, whether our bus on the other side would wait for us, nor how long it would take to get to Livingstone airport, from which we were to fly to Johannesburg and on to Cape Town. You can imagine how itchy we got! I, finally, implored the manager of Kubu to take us in one of their cars to the ferry station, but when we were just ready to hop into their car, the Wilderness guy showed up. Needless to say, we expressed our extreme unhappiness. But he got us down there, we cleared emigration speedily, and a little speedboat ferried just the two of us across the broad expanse of the river, were the bus was still waiting for us.

Thus our safari ended on a hectic and confused note, but I can only say: We did get to see what are called the Big Five in Africa: lion, elephant, rhino, buffalo, and leopard, although, had it not come to pass, it would have been also okay. Our guides and trackers everywhere we came tried very hard to find them for us. But what I also relish is, that I got to see one of the Little Five, the elephant shrew!

From the Namib to the Okavango and Beyond

Via Zambia to the Cape Peninsula.

Part 3

June 25 to 28, 2005

Ten years ago we had safaried in Zimbabwe and enjoyed our trip very much, but with Mugabe having brought his country closer to civil strife, we didn't care to enter it. Otherwise, our ongoing flight would have been from Victoria Falls to Johannesburg and on to Cape Town. We were therefore to fly out of Livingstone in Zambia.

The ferry station on the Zambian side was very crowded; lots of traffic between Botswana and Zambia. They sure could use a bridge there. The driver of the little bus that was to bring us to Livingstone was waiting for us at the landing site of the motorboat that had delivered us from Botswana and helped us to get speedily through Zambian immigration. Then it was off on an asphalt road, but alongside it, we saw the "old" Africa we knew from our travels in Kenia and Tanzania in the mid-eigthies. Only recently has Zambia risen from poor government and now still has a way to go.

Let me mention here that neither Botswana nor South Africa get foreign aid, as such being the only African countries. In Botswana diamonds were found right when it became independent from being a British protectorate. These finds support its economy. On the other side, Namibia has been the greatest recipient of German foreign aid of any African country. Ha! I wonder whether it's because of the Schutztruppe's massacre of the Hereros at the Waterberg in the early 1900rds, when German settlers desired their grazing lands? Several years ago, the Namibian government filed a lawsuit in the USA for compensation from Germany for the Hereros' sufferings (who else will yet ask for compensation?), but were advised by US attorneys, that success was unlikely. So it got squashed.

After an hour's drive we arrived at the Livingstone airport. From there a South African Nationwide Airlines Boeing 727 got us to Joburg. After takeoff, when the plane banked, I could see from my center seat the Victoria Falls. 'The Smoke

That Thunders', as the falls were and still are called by the natives before Livingstone of Stanley's "Dr. Livingstone, I presume?" fame, discovered them for the world and named them for Queen Victoria. Ten years ago, when we had stayed in the town of Victoria Falls, we had visited these magnificent falls three times in one day, plus had taken a helicopter flight over them.

I gradually entered into a conversation with my aisle seat neighbor, which evolved into one of the most vibrant flight conversations I've ever had, with both of us remarking upon arrival at Joburg how quickly the almost three hour flight had passed. He was a professor of education from Adelaide University in Australia, coming from an international conference on education in Lusaka, Zambia, its capital. Instead of flying, he had opted for a seven hour bus ride from Lusaka to Livingstone and said, "It was the experience of a life time". I believed him! Towards landing, I mentioned that I rarely wish anyone Good Luck, but rather Success at whatever they are doing. Also, that I love to say, "You be good", which almost all people so addressed construe as to be morally good – which it could be – but more so meaning, to be good at what you're doing! We briefly saw each other across some distance in the terminal and with a wave of his hand I heard, "You be good". Either I must have been bad – or we had made Contact. And we had never even mentioned our names!

From the Cape Town airport a van of Thompson Travel delivered us to the four star Portswood Hotel, where two liveried doormen greeted us, one of them taking us to our nice room. Only with a security card issued to us upon check-in were we allowed to enter the elevator.

The following morning we were picked up by a Thompson van for our Cape Peninsula tour. From other hotels four more people joined us. One was a couple from Brazil, their English not very good, but she speaking German. So I got into some translations along the way. The others were two Canadian women, who had just finished volunteering in northern Mozambique for MMI, am interdenominational   US/Canadian organization which gathers volunteer doctors from across the world to dispatch them to developing countries for ophthalmic surgery and dental work. The two women, Marty and Ila, had paid their own fare to assist the medical professionals. Marty was 80 years old and a very spunky woman. I became very much endeared to her. When I found out about their work, I mentioned my meeting with Rudolf Dausab in Namibia and the need there for medical care of this kind. She handed me a little brochure with MMI's addresses. More about this later.

Our tour took us along the gorgeous shoreline, very much reminiscent of Big Sur in California, just more settled. I think it's a good place to live. It has a pleasant climate and all the conveniences of the First World. We entered the nature preserve at the lower tip which is populated, incongruously, by introduced ostriches, zebras, and Cape baboons, the latter supposedly very aggressive when they smell food. We never saw any of them though.

Somewhere, there stood a memorial to Barthomoleu Dias, the Portuguese seafarer. Being the first European to sight the Cape in 1480. He called it the Cape of Storms. Alas, his superior, the Portuguese king, Henry the Navigator, who never 'navigated' anywhere, didn't want his explorers frightened off by such a name – remember the Portuguese were out to get to the Spice Islands in Indonesia, to shortcut the Arabs who either dominated or blocked the trade in spices from the Far East. So, Henry had it called The Cape of Good Hope. And this it became. Then, Vasco da Gama rounded the Cape in 1497. The rest is history.

We stopped at a sign proclaimed here to be the most southwesterly point of the African continent, the Cape of Good Hope. Nearby Ute had to pick up a couple of pebbles as souvenirs; one for a friend and one for us. Pssst! A drive with an aerial tram brought us to the top of a hill and the southernmost lighthouse of the African continent with a 360° view.

Then, following our request, our driver dropped us off at a seafood restaurant where Ute and I enjoyed an excellent seafood luncheon, except that our Brazilian man had to have a steak. A bit later, on a subsequent stop at a beach cove, a breeding group of jackass penguins performed their antics.

In a slight drizzle we walked Kirstenbosch, the magnificent botanical garden of Cape Town, resplendent with its many proteas. And with all good things having to come to an end, we were finally dropped off at our respective hotels again. Later, Ute and I walked, what's called, The Waterfront, part harbor, part shopping area, ranging from the mundane to the exquisite. The most interesting section was a co-op where we just couldn't help buying a few more things – now that we didn't have to watch our 25 pound luggage limit any longer. The waterfront is a redevelopment of the area in which the owners of the Portswood Hotel, where we stayed, were very much involved; one can just walk across a street to get there. And since everyone in southern Africa drives on the 'wrong side' of the road, we had to remember to first look to the right, then to the left, very difficult when you are habituated to doing the opposite. But people drove very disciplined and courteous. They stopped, even if we looked the 'wrong way'.

Of the people at The Waterfront, in the shops, stalls, and restaurants, their skin color ranged in a continuum from white to dark brown, a true representation of the multihued colors of the South African flag. At least there, one gained the impression as 'if it could be made to work'. One could find Nelson Mandela mementos in many places, and Robben Island, where he spent many years imprisoned, is clearly visible from Cape Town. It is more than a wonder, that a man who was incarcerated for 28 years, was able to retain his humanity and thus greatly contribute to a peaceful transition from Apartheid to the present South Africa. From all the people we had the opportunity to speak with, whether van drivers, shop keepers, waiters, and hotel personnel, no matter if black or white, or anywhere in between, we gained the impression of a cautious confidence in the future of their country. May they succeed!

The Waterfront is a very vibrant, alive place to walk, also secure, which some areas in Cape Town supposedly are not. Again and again, we walked through the many kinds of stores, even if only to see what we might have missed before, or to see again. Crossing a plaza, we saw a black man in coverall sitting on a stone bench, playing with a cat I thought might be a stray. Ute, always drawn to cats, had to go there to pet her. The man, a sailor on leave, was the owner of this beautifully colored and patterned being.

The next day we were picked up for our half day city tour and, lo and behold, there were Marty and Ila again. Our first stop was at the old fort built by the Dutch settlers. Our driver, of Malay ethnic background – the Malays were once brought to the Cape by the Dutch as slaves, since the local Bushmen or Hottentots were disinclined to do slave labor – took us to where District 6 had once been. This had been a vibrant multiethnic neighborhood, razed during the Apartheid regime. A church, that had to be left standing, nowadays commemorates the events of

147

its bulldozing in the early 1900rds. There, we learned, that it had just been decided to rename South Africa's capital, Pretoria, named after an Afrikaner, to Tshwane, meaning 'We are the same'. This renaming has been going on all over the world where colonial powers either renamed or corrupted the pronunciation of native names. It is an expression of independence from the past. While I can understand it, I must also question the issue when it pertains to locales that have been established or became known to the larger world only through the efforts of the old Western powers. An example would be the name of the city of Cape Town, even of Victoria Falls.

And Table Mountain, the close, magnificent backdrop of Cape Town, was still waiting for us. At times, it was obscured by clouds, but when we finally took the aerial tram up, which they call a funicular down there, most clouds had dissipated and we had a magnificent view of Cape Town below. That evening Ute and I had to try a Cape Malay meal at the Portswood restaurant. It had been highly recommended to us, both the cuisine and the restaurant's expertise in preparing it. While some of it was good, we both are partial to Thai and Indonesian cooking. Ah, well.

Then it was time to say good bye to Cape Town, where I could see myself to live or, actually, the Cape Peninsula – if I were reborn. The city's proximal backdrop of mountains, Table Mountain, Lion's Head, and Signal Hill are magnificent. While we waited in the hotel lobby for our pickup by Thompson to be taken to the airport, one of the two doormen, apparently of Malay background stood with us. We had talked on and off with him leaving or returning to the hotel. He had a very dignified demeanor. Ute had caught his manner, his sense of being, well before me. When she pointed it out, I too noticed the 'peace' the man seemed to project. At one time he mention being Muslim. I have this almost lifelong bias against Islam, dating back to my north African trip in 1956, but have never held it against individuals of this persuasion. When he had joined us, I stood up from the chair to stand with him. When he urged me to sit down: No need to stand with him, I told him I had joined him standing to honor him. "I need not be honored", was his response. My retort was, "We all need to be honored". We talked about 'balance', balance in all things, and I argued that in addition to balance, we also need imbalance, striving, going for things, and I requoted to him a line from a poem I had written years ago for myself, called 'Belonging'. In a line I state, that I am Western Man by intellect.

148

Upon my urging for imbalance, in addition to balance, we shook hands on his initiative. I gave him our card and he said, "You'll hear from me." By snailmail, I asked? His name is Tariq. That's all I know and need to know of this doorman!

We had to take this dreadfully long trip of four flight segments from Cape Town to Atlanta, the one from Joburg to Atlanta with a stop again at Ilha del Sal lasting 22-1/2 hours, then the two hour shuttle ride to Prescott, which we barely caught. From bed-to-bed it took us 47 hours. A killer!

But I promised 'more later', an ending that took place only two weeks after our return. Remember, Marty had given me a pamphlet on the organization she and her companion had been with in Mozambique. Having come back, I had misplaced it, but when I found it again, I called their headquarters in Allen, Texas. Remember, too, Rudolf and Ouma Lydia in Namibia and her vision problems?

I had a good chat with their operator, who told me that their Director of International Operations was currently in Peru, assembling a team of doctors and medical personnel to treat locals with ophthalmic and dental problems, meaning surgery. I gave her my email address, etc., and within half an hour I received an email from Brian Piecuch in Peru acknowledging my inquiry, the inquiry being, whether his organization could send a team to the Topnaar people in Namibia. And since I gave him in a two hour email exchange also Rudolf Dausab's email address in Namibia, he contacted him directly, telling him, that MMI requires an invitation from the locals to come. Also that they need to investigate the accommodation and feeding of the medical team. Preparations to assemble and dispatch a medical team may take up to two years. So, now it is in Rudolf's hands to find out what he can arrange down there. Maybe Ute and I will get to Namibia once more after all.

But now my account has come full circle. What I had told Rudolf already in the dunes south of Walvis Bay: It's all about contacts.

Journey to Sumatra

March 1990

Sumatra – sixth-largest island in the world – home to elephants, rhinos, tigers and orang utans – what is left of them, due to human population growth. One of the largest tribal communities are the Batak people with five million being of the Lutheran faith.

In 1903, Karl Weissenbruch, my wife, Ute's, grandfather journeyed to the Lake Toba Region on Sumatra as a missionary. In 1906, following the wedding ceremony, his newlywed's horse shied upon their departure for home, being pursued by a tiger. Fortunately, the tiger was unsuccessful in his hunt, or my wife would not have been born in Tarutung, Sumatra, in late 1936.

Three years later, when Germany invaded Holland, the Dutch interned all Axis civilians, Germans, Austrians and Italians, in their Indonesian colony. My wife's father was arrested on the road and his car confiscated. He was shipped to Dehra Dun at the foothills of the Himalayas, the Allied collection center for Axis civilians living in Southeast Asian, where he was interned for the next seven years until his return to Germany in 1946.

My wife's mother with her three children, was interned on Sumatra until the Japanese invasion in 1942. The Japanese, members of the Axis, 'liberated' the family, who, at first received no living support, and was moved into one of the vacated Dutch homes. Following the growth of the Indonesian resistance movement against the Dutch colonial masters after the War, the family was also shipped back to Germany in 1947. Four years thereafter, Ute and I met for the first time. Nine years later we married, and three years on emigrated to Canada and eventually to the USA.

Some time in 1989 I suggested to my wife that we visit her Sumatran roots. When her parents had returned to Sumatra in the 1960s, where her father lectured at a Batak university, her post-war-born sister, Dörthe, had lived with her parents there for several years. She and her husband were very much interested in visiting Sumatra, and so it transpired that we planned a trip there, Dörthe and her husband were to come from Berlin and we from Chicago, to meet in Singapore. Dörthe had brushed up on

150

her knowledge of the Indonesian language, Bahasa Indonesia, and was to be our translator.

In late January Ute and I flew United from Chicago via San Francisco and Tokyo to Singapore. We had upgraded to business class, when, on one of the legs, sitting on the starboard side, we became aware of being nearly the only passengers there, while on the port side many more seats were occupied. Then I recalled that United had, two weeks earlier on another 747 flight, lost several passengers from business class. This was the result of an improperly closed cargo door on the starboard side that had sprung open in flight and had torn open the fuselage. Some passengers along with their seats were sucked out over the Pacific. After some consideration, we decided not to cut our sojourn to Indonesia short and moved over to port side.

We roamed Singapore for a day, then met with our relatives to fly to Medan on Sumatra. On arrival, I dickered with one of the taxi drivers in front of the airport for a decent fare to take us to a motel-restaurant in Pematang Siantar, where I had made reservations. The ride introduced us to a strange, foreign world of left-hand-side traffic, a chaos of all kinds of vehicles, honking for numerous reasons, the air pervaded by two-stroke engine fumes, vendor stalls lining the road, and people, especially children, everywhere.

The motel, where my wife's parents had dined frequently, turned out to be very nice and was air-conditioned. In the morning we enjoyed a typical Indonesian breakfast of strong coffee, nasi goreng (fried rice), and bami goreng (fried noodles), passion fruit juice and papaya. Then we left for a bank to exchange our currencies for wads of Indonesian rupees. The armed but friendly guards outside the bank asked for their picture to be taken, just as many of the children and adults on our later sojourn did. Thereafter, we visited the President of Nommensen University, a former student of my father-in-law, who invited us for breakfast with his wife the next morning.

In the afternoon Dörthe and Ute went to purchase a durian, a green, oval, tropical tree fruit about the size of a foot. It had several one-inch diameter pits imbedded in a white, creamy flesh. It looked good, the two women relished it, and even Günter took to it! I thought to myself: "try everything once", even if this delight smelled like a rotting corpse to me. After this first and only experience, I took a deep breath every time I had to pass by the huge piles of durian, stacked by street vendors, in order to

151

quickly leave the terrible odor behind – many of the merchants giving me a knowing grin, for there are only lovers and haters of durian! That evening we enjoyed a delicious exotic dinner, as we did many times thereafter, always consumed with beer, following the motto "don't drink the water". The problem was that beer came only in liter bottles.

Someone at the university recommended a Muslim Batak, who owned a well-kept van, to drive us, when called, for a number of days to the various places we intended to visit in the vicinity of Lake Toba. Then we took off from Siantar to Parapat, the world's largest volcanic lake. It is a so-called wet caldera, about 100 km long, 30 km wide, and 500 m deep, the remnant of a mega volcano that erupted approximately 75,000 years ago, possibly the largest in 25 million years. Because of its location near the equator, from where jet streams distributed the immense amount of volcanic material thrown into the atmosphere, it caused a massive climate-change, a volcanic winter, and may have reduced the human population and life in general. A resurgent dome formed the large Samosir Island, which is today sprinkled with villages and vacation resorts. The elevation of 900 m makes for a pleasantly cooler climate.

Parapat is dirty with a lot of garbage strewn about. When, in earlier times, the natives used plant material for wrapping and eating, tossed discards rotted away – not so with today's plastics. A sense of ecology and recycling is yet to develop. The next day, after some negotiating, which reduced our fare from 10,000 rupees to 3,000, we boarded the ferry from Parapat to Samosir. On the half-hour boat ride two Chinese teenage boys practiced their English, quizzing me intensely about the Western World. From our simple but comfortable hotel the view across the lake was incredibly beautiful. After next morning's breakfast a walk took us to a couple of Batak villages for a little shopping, then to view some old Batak grave sites. Thereafter, we returned to our hotel, followed by a swim in the crystal-clear and refreshing waters of the lake. In the evening, we participated in a special dinner for 40 people from around the world, with the exception of Americans. The dinner was followed by a group of song performers, all hotel employees. Bataks love to sing, and these people were good.

The next morning we headed for Balige, another village with familial background. After our driver picked us up, we soon left the touristy area behind, seeing more of the old-type Batak

152

campongs, steeple-roofed buildings, where people lived 'upstairs', their animals fenced-in, 'downstairs.' These settlements of maybe six to eight houses were surrounded by an earthen mound with trees and bamboo growing along its ridge for protection against wild animals. Only two gates at each end offered access to a *campong*.

We visited family friends in Balige and the church built by grandfather Weissenbruch. Our stay in a Batak guesthouse introduced us to the customary bathroom facilities. Everything was sparkling clean; a hole in the tiled floor represented the toilet and a two by two foot wide and four foot high tiled basin held cold water with a ladle serving to douse and clean oneself.

A side trip took us to Sitorang, a tiny village in the hills. Arriving there, we were, as everywhere, quickly surrounded by children, delighting by the sight of Westerners. Then, a man, approximately 50 to 60 years old, showed up, clad in a sarong. When Dörthe explained the reason for our visit, her grandfather having once lived here, the man, to our surprise, told us that his grandfather had once provided the place for her grandfather to build his house. He led us around, but no remnants of a structure could be seen anymore. Later, in Chicago, when we viewed Ute's pictures of this encounter, we saw that the man had changed the location of where he wore his sarong many times during our tour, at one time wearing it even on his head.

Here is another true story about sarongs. The Dutch had been in the Indonesian islands for a couple of centuries, but conquered Bali only at the very beginning of the 20th century. When the Dutch Royal couple came for their first visit to newly acquired Bali, the Dutch authorities asked the local village chiefs to make sure that the women, who would be lining the Royal couple's route, cover their breasts, which was at the time still uncommon. Well, they did – in a fashion. It is told that when the Royal couple's carriage passed by groups, the women simply lifted their sarongs to cover up the offending breasts. They knew how to get back at their conquerors!

Once again, we were driven through the neighborhoods of Lake Toba, stopping at old villages where we were invited into some houses. There were children everywhere. One old woman said she had 13! Usually, people we met were very friendly. An old Karo King building, now a museum, had housed 13 generations of 'kings', each with up to 22 wives and up to 117 children. The sturdily built structure stood on approximately 10 foot tall, solid poles as a protection from tigers and other wild beasts. The 'king' slept at its front, from where a door led to the women's quarters, each having their own fire place and bamboo pipe water supply, all guarded by a castrated servant. Refuse was apparently dropped through the gaps between the horizontal poles.

Our ride took us to Brastagi. My wife remembered the two volcanos nearby, the Sibayah and Sinagan, both dormant. Indonesia, being located on the Pacific Rim of Fire, has 76 active volcanos, in addition to its many dormant ones. After some searching, we found the house her family had lived in after they had been freed from internment. Nothing had really changed in decades. In her her childhood, Ute had so often walked the long driveway to and from the house and walked through a nearby 'canyon' to school – now she was returned to being a little girl.

Our accommodation in town was the Bukit Kubu motel, an old colonial structure on a beautifully manicured garden. The next morning our driver did not show up. I had paid him on a daily basis, given him even some extra money. The previous night I did not have exact cash, which is why I asked my wife to pay him. So, what was his reason for abandoning us? Had he made enough money; did he get tired of chauffeuring us around, or was his Muslim sensitivity injured by having been paid by a woman? No matter, we found ready transportation. In the meantime we visited a nature preserve with many old and different trees, a market with much too muddy pathways, but a multitude of fruit and dried fish, the latter sorted by size, from 2 inches to 15 inches, in big baskets. Then there was a beautiful waterfall and hot springs. On a walk through fields we saw the biggest cabbages we have ever seen.

A taxi driver suggested taking us to a village of Karo Bataks for a native dance, celebrating the exchange of police chiefs. It sounded interesting, and we took off – to a place far removed from Western customs and yet, not its trappings. We were the only Westerners and were greeted by the two police chiefs, their wives, and the village elders, then invited to partake in their common dinner. This being a Muslim community, the women ate separate from the men, while our two wives were allowed to sit cross-legged with us and the men. Before dinner, small water bowls were passed around to wash fingers. Dinner, which was served on waxed brown paper, consisted of rice with one piece of meat and a couple of vegetable pieces on top, tasty

154

and spicy, all eaten by hand. I surreptitiously admonish my wife, a lefty, to change hands for eating, since the left hand is considered the 'dirty' one. After the meal we were invited to sit in the front row of benches, together with the 'big shots', to watch the forthcoming dance on a raised stage. It had turned night. More and more people from other villages drifted in, and with Indonesians having narrower personal space, we were soon tightly surrounded by humanity. Electric lights then illuminated the stage and various groups of old and young danced, speeches were held, and a lone singer performed. Eventually, six professional male and female dancers with incredible grace and agility entered the stage. Some of the postures of their dance must have conveyed some meaning, unknown to us, for the audience broke at various times into laughter. Then we were invited onstage to dance with the 'professionals.' After some hesitation we agreed, but in no way were we able to match the grace of these men and women. Did we hear some subdued snickers from the huge, but polite crowd? Eventually, after I had handed over a donation for the village, we slipped away and our taxi took us back to the motel, which we now found completely occupied by noisy Chinese.

The Chinese New Year is not celebrated on one day only, but over a number of days. There is a large Chinese population living in Indonesia, and these visitors had driven up from low-elevation, humid Medan to the higher-elevation, and thus cooler Brastagi to celebrate New Year. And the celebration went on through the entire night! People talking, radios blaring, children screaming – were they never going to stop? Our plans were to rise early in the morning and climb the Sibayak volcano, but sleep was impossible. Towards morning, Dörthe came to our room, telling us that her husband was unable to sleep and was ready to leave right now for Berlin. Ute handed her two Benadryll, suggesting she give them to her husband to relax and sleep for what was left of the night. When my wife asked her sister the next morning whether Günter had been able to sleep having taken the pills, she was told: "He did not want to swallow the pills, I did. I slept!"

Our neighbors in the next room were especially noisy, and I thought putting some brakes on their activities. Recalling an old trick to silence noisy next-door motel room neighbors, I got my pocket knife out and wrapped one end in some insulating clothing. Then I partially pulled out an electric plug from the wall of our room adjoining their unit, put the knife-back across the poles and – bang! – not only did the radio and lights next door go off, but the electrical supply for the entire motel complex of three buildings went dead. Unfortunately, there must have been a master circuit breaker; the lights were on again a few minutes later. The Chinese did not stop their noises for even a second! When we finished our sleepless night and stepped outside, the pleasantly manicured motel grounds had become a total mess.

Rather bedraggled, we left early for our volcanic ascent. The trail eventually led through, what looked like jungle, but people lived within it. Then we passed by a giant, staked down water buffalo. Günter had always displayed some caution with animals, which is why I thought I would demonstrate that there was nothing to be afraid of. Thus, I approached the buffalo, thinking to pet him. About eight feet from the creature, I heard a subdued growl with one eye of the creature eyeing me. I figured that, maybe, eight feet was close enough to demonstrate courage, and backed away. Just when we were to go on, a loin-cloth-clad boy of about five years old, appeared from the bushes, pulled out the stake, and led the beast away. Did I feel foolish? Of course not, because the two knew each other.

The trail eventually turned into a very steep concrete stairway dating back to Dutch colonial times. There is this story of my mother-in-law ascending these very steps in the 1960s with a small group of Western women. Suddenly, several Batak teenage boys, intent on relieving the women of their valuables, approached them. Despite being Christians or Muslims, Bataks are beholden by ancestor worship. With my mother-in-law fluent in the Batak language and knowledgeable of the customs, she now assaulted the youth with a flood of Batak admonishions about what their ancestors would think of such behavior. And, lo and behold, shamed, the boys quickly disappeared into the surrounding woods.

Climbing on, we eventually reached the tree line where the old steps ended and new ones had been laid, which showed however early signs of deterioration. Not much farther, we reached a group of laborers building more concrete steps, using the local gritty, volcanic material, containing lots of sulfur. The result was that the new-formed steps fell apart as quickly as they were built. We reached the nearly 200 m wide caldera and walked down into it. Sulfuric vapors were escaping from multiple vents, from which the natives tried to catch the sulfur by affixing burlap bags over the major outlets. Ute took some close-up pictures, only to find later that some of her camera's metal parts had been slightly corroded. We descended an extremely muddy path, but only after Ute had fallen and become rather muddy, and I then cut us some walking sticks, did we make it, three-legged, down the mountain.

I had wanted to bring a Batak sword home, thinking I could get it diagonally into my suitcase; and I found one, except that it turned out to be too long. Well, the handle of my suitcase had been torn, so I thought to purchase a new suitcase of appropriate size in Medan. There, in a modern department store, I did find one. While I stood at the check-out counter, I suddenly felt the hair on my left arm being pulled. Turning around, I faced two Chinese teenage girls smiling at me, one of them still holding onto that small blond tuft. Aware why she was doing it – that Asians are less hairy than we throwback Caucasians – I simply smiled back and turned around again, as she let go. But then I felt another tug. The other girl also had to aquatint herself with this peculiar characteristic.

Prior to our departure, we explored Medan a bit, a city of over one million people. Then, after our wives had acquired some sticky-rice pastry, we retired to a hotel lobby for some coffee and pastry. It was utterly delicious. Despite the traffic-fume saturated streets, Günter was prepared to brave the streets once more simply to fetch a second helping of these delicacies. And he did!

Then, our flight took us to Bali, a distance almost as great as crossing the United States from west to east, truly so, if one would fly from Aceh on Sumatra's western tip all the way to Indonesia's eastern extent. We spent a pleasant week there in a guesthouse suggested by my sister in Germany, living only in our purchased sarongs. Eventually, we parted, our relatives staying on for a few more days, while we made our way to Chicago. Of course, Chicago was socked in again by a snowstorm, so that our flight had to be rerouted to Omaha, adding a few more hours to an already too long flight. Eventually, though, Chicago had us back after our memorable, tropical sojourn, where we had found friendly people and beautiful nature.

157

Excursions in Saxony's Switzerland

October 2007

One hundred million years ago an ocean began to cover large parts of Europe. For fifteen million years streams and rivers eroded the islands and surrounding elevations, carrying mainly quartz sand to the ocean's bottom, depositing this material, layer by layer, close to 600 meters deep. In time these layers were compressed to gray marine sandstone. These stone layers, from 20 to 120 meters thick, are interspersed by clay layers up to 4 meters thick. Clay was laid down early on, so that thicker sandstone layers dominate the upper layers. Subsequent uplifts created vertical cracks in the stone. Sandstone, being permeable, allows rainwater to penetrate downwards until it is stopped by an impermeable clay layer which directs it sideways until the water finds an exit.

When the ocean's waters finally retreated and erosion of the sandstone masses by rain and the Elbe River began, the vertical cracks and the particular layering created a wild landscape of table mountains, spires, towers, needles and ridges, with clefts, narrow, steep canyons and small valleys. Were they not covered nowadays by forests and undergrowth these formations would be reminiscent of Monument Valley.

Beginning in the stone age, men built defensible positions on some of the peaks and table mountains, such as the mighty, never conquered Fortress Koenigstein. Other such elevations feature inns where the hiker can delight in one of Saxony's specialties, Sauerbraten with red cabbage and dumplings, washing them down with a stein of beer or some good Saxonian wine. From these heights we enjoyed far-reaching views across this so varied landscape – my wife, myself, together with our sister and brother-in-law. One of these table mountains, the Bastei, once an ancient mountain bastion, high above the Elbe river, even sports a hotel which can be reached by car.

For the hiker seeking simpler pleasures, many a promontory offers a place for a snack or sack lunch. Looking down a couple of hundred meters may be forested valleys or freshly plowed fields, others showing the tender green of recently sown winter-wheat. Nearby or in the distance, other rock formations and outcrops may be visible. For the knowledgeable, mushrooms grow everywhere throughout the surrounding forests.

While some of the trails are level, most have steep elevation differences. The area's trails are maintained by the national park service. To overcome slopes with wooden beams providing stairways. When the trails pass through canyons, ravines and gorges, they become stairs and ladders of aluminum. In some of the wildest parts, there are steel rails or handles solidly imbedded in rock. We appreciated these handholds most when we descended the Wilde Hoelle (Wild Hell), a convoluted, narrow canyon which the normal hiker would be unable to cross without the handholds. Many a promontory would be inaccessible without the stairs and ladders.

On one of our excursions, our trail passed through several gorges along numerous stairways. Eventually, we had climbed up on ladders to the top of the Schrammsteine (Scarred Rocks). Then, being uncomfortable with the height, I climbed down to a lower flat area from where three trails departed. While I had a snack there, a large group of about twenty people came up the ladder, all looking like hikers, but some were carrying fancy photographic equipment. They took a break from their climb right in front of me. Suddenly, I did a double-take. There, not three paces distant, being part of this group, stood the German President, Horst Koehler with his wife Luise. My wife, having come down by then, got very busy snapping his picture. While there are some substantial differences, imagine George and Barbara Bush climbing up there!

Among many other hikes, their ups and downs straining our calf muscles, we also took a silent, leisurely, oar-powered boat trip through the narrow canyon of the dammed Kirnitzsch River, a tributary of the Elbe River. Another excursion on one of the old side-paddle steamers brought us to the town of Rathen by the Elbe . Started in 1836, the Saxon Steamship Company is the oldest steamship company in the world with the most paddle wheelers and ships. From Rathen, which features the Karl-May-Festival, we hiked up the Bastei Mountain to view the remnants of its ancient fortification and looked way-down to the Elbe River where a paddle-wheeler was making its way upstream.

Dresden, Saxony's capital, was only an hour's drive away from our small A-frame vacation home in the village of Lichtenhain. On February 13, 1945, in a night air raid, the British leveled this ancient city, Dresden, with its many historic buildings causing a death toll of 30,000. The American writer, Kurt Vonnegut, experienced this event as an American POW. In 1969 his novel, Slaughterhouse Five, was published in which his literary alter ego, Billy Pilgrim, portrays Vonnegut's personal gruesome experience.

Today, much, but by far not all, has been rebuilt and restored – 44 years of communist rule were not conducive to the city's restoration. Today, Dresden, once again, has become a vibrant city featuring, among many other world-renowned historic buildings, the Zwinger, the Semper Opera House, and the Frauenkirche.

Our final day took us to the town of Radebeul where Germany's most successful writer, Karl May, had his residence. Between 1878 and 1910 he penned more than 80 novels and short stories dealing with the American West, the Orient, and other locales around the world, only some of which he visited towards the the latter part of his life. Most were travel and adventure stories of his imagination, but usually well researched. His residence and the adjacent Villa Bearfat hold possibly the the most extensive collection of Indian artifacts in Germany. A large diorama depicts the details of Custer's battle at the Little Bighorn. His writings did popularize the American West with the German public. Generations of youngsters grew up reading his adventure stories. Since little was translated into English, although into many other languages, I have made it my task to translate a number of his "Western" novels into English.

Finally, we entered the city of Meissen, where Johann Friedrich Boettger invented in the early seventeen hundreds the process of manufacturing porcelain which, until then, had to be imported from China, where the process had originally been discovered. From Meissen it, eventually, spread across the world.

In the Albrecht's Castle we admired the architecture and huge paintings of the Romantic period of the 18th century, depicting events from German history. It has been the seat of many Saxon kings. Its construction was begun by the first German King, Henry I, former Duke of Saxony, chosen by his peers in 919 AD.

The cries of large flocks of migrating geese and cranes overhead called on us to journey on. Two hours later we arrived in Berlin.

Zambezi

July 1997

Africa's third-largest river, the Zambesi, its source located in the mountains of Angola, flows almost straight east, eventually discharging its waters into the Indian Ocean, on the shores of Mozambique.

In 1997, when Zimbabwe's economy, once one of the richest in Africa, and its social fabric had not yet been destroyed by the megalomaniac Mugabe and his cohorts, my wife, Ute, and I took a safari there. We flew from the capital city of Harare to the town of Kariba, on the eastern tip of Lake Kariba, where the Zambesi had been dammed in 1959, and from there took a boat to our first wilderness camp somewhere on the lake shore.

The center of the tented camp was the communal area with the kitchen. On one side individual tents had been pitched, while on the opposite side stood the shower and toilet facility. The shower stall was open towards the lake, so that one could enjoy the shower and view simultaneously. When a guest expressed the desire to take a shower, hot water was prepared and poured into a bucket suspended over the shower head.

Our two evenings there were spent gathering around the campfire, called bush TV. We were three couples traveling with Wilderness Travel, Christa and Steve from Chicago, Debby and Steve from Glendale, AZ, and the two of us from Prescott, AZ. In addition to various other instructions, our safari guide, Patrick, explained that, if we had to go to the loo at night, a walk of about 300 feet, we should not only shine the flashlight down before us, but also scan the surrounding bushes for eye reflections from animals hiding there. When Christa asked, "And what do I do, should I see eyes?" our guide told her, "Call Herbert." Problem solved!

Bush walks took us into the surrounding countryside, where we had to walk in a queue, with our guide leading, his high-powered rifle shouldered. We quickly learned if the air was clear, or if big game was nearby. Was there a possible threat, the rifle moved from his shoulder to his hand.

Returning to Kariba, we took another small aircraft to Mana Pools, a World Heritage Site, because of its rich wildlife and scenery. It is located just south of the Zambezi River.

Driven to the river, four canoes were waiting for us. The subcontractors for the three day canoe ride down river were a young white Zimbabwean couple. She, looking terrible due to multiple bouts of malaria. While travelers can take prophylactics for malaria, all-year residents cannot and must take what comes. She, together with three native helpers, would drive along the river to set up each evening's camp prior to our arrival.

Her husband was going to join us on our river trip. Since my wife and I had canoed many times in Minnesota and Ontario, we were looking forward to this experience, but just when we boarded our canoe, a black park guard wanted to take over the helm. No way was I going to permit this, thus the 'poor' man had to sit in the middle, with Ute up front. At least I was diplomatic enough not to point out to him that, had this trip taken place a hundred years earlier, he would certainly have sat where the work had to be done.

Before taking off, we were informed that we would pass about 50 hippopotamuses per kilometer on our three days of about 40 km total, which meant a proud, or should I say, scary, total of 2000. Hippos are highly territorial, and on land, when they come out to graze in the night, kill the most people of any big African animal. We pushed off, always staying close to the riverbanks and far away from hippo pods. Except for one occasion, when a hippos suddenly surfaced near one of our canoes, we did not encounter any dangerous situations.

For lunch breaks, we stopped along the river bank, where we were provided with delicious sandwiches from the cooler. Aside from the many hippos, we saw eagles, cranes, and three foot long monitor lizards, scouting the river bank for bird eggs and small prey. We also saw various species of antelope, one of which was the water buck. This big, gray antelope has a white oval ring on its derriere, and the story goes that its progenitor happened to sit on a freshly painted toilet seat, thus the ring. Then there were all sizes of crocodiles and, at times, some elephants crossing the river. When the water level rose above their bodies, they raised their trunks like snorkels. Several species of king fishers were darting along the river, or sitting patiently on a branch overhanging the water. When they would spot a small fish, the would dive down, snatch it and bring it up to their perch, where they whacked the fish on a branch to kill it, and then swallow it headfirst.

The Zambezi is a braided stream, not channeled as many Western rivers. This means that, at times, we traveled through a sea of grass and reeds, where the water became so shallow that our guides had to push us through. The afternoons were the most pleasant, when we got closer to our day's destination. Instead of paddling, we brought our canoes side-by-side and held them loosely together. Then the cooler was opened, and we enjoyed either a cold beer or a chilled glass of wine. Culture and civilization on the Zambezi! Dinner on our first evening was memorable. A large table had been expertly set up under big overhanging branches of a giant tree, next to the riverbank. The table could not have been arranged any better at a five-star restaurant in Europe or the U.S., with dinner and company highly enjoyable. A full moon had risen, its light reflecting from the gently murmuring waters, and, lo and behold, there was a second reflection on the water – the light of bright Venus. All of this was accompanied by the whines, howls and 'laughter' of a hyena on the opposite river bank, which was part of Zambia.

Arriving at our day's destination, our camp was all set up, our laundry was returned, and we gathered for a sun-downer, a drink of our choice – but without ice. Unbelievingly, a flush toilet was set up, and a shower was waiting. Our hosts carried a huge round tub for the preparation of hot water. Worried, I asked whether it served also as a cannibal pot? When at night, my wife and I had to visit the loo, we did it together, but never encountered a wild beast.

On the eve of our third day, we arrived at Chikwenya Lodge, managed by our guide's wife. It consisted of several large, permanent tents, serving as living and sleeping rooms. Joining each was a man-high masonry structure with the sanitary facilities, wash basin, flush toilet and shower. With lions and elephants occasionally passing through the camp at night, one could step on a small stool to look over the masonry wall and watch the beasts go by. A huge dinner table, for at least twelve people, stood under giant trees, and the candelabra in its center had been built tall enough so that everyone was able to see across the table unimpeded, when conversing with each other. The lodge's symbol was the bee-eater, a small colorful bird living in flocks, which build their nests by pecking holes into the clay of the river bank.

Depending on the guests' desire, they were driven mornings or afternoons to established hides in the surrounding area, from where one could, in silence, observe the wildlife passing by. On the riverbank, these were crocs, lazing in the sun, also buffalo, elephants and baboons coming to drink. Bush walks took us to inland lagoons, remnants from the rainy season or flooding. By the time we were there, many had become large mud holes. One of them held the carcass of an old bull hippo, likely defeated by a younger rival, then expelled from the pod and to die from his injuries. On one hike, we came to the biggest baobab tree we ever saw. Twelve people would probably have had difficulties encircling it. The baobab is also called the 'upside down tree', since its branches, when not in leaf, look like roots.

We had to leave this magical place and fly to Victoria Falls, so named by Livingstone for Queen Victoria, when he 'discovered' them in 1855. Of course, he made them 'only' known to the world; the natives knew them for a long time, calling them Mosi-oa-Tunya, the Smoke-that-Thunders. And thunder they do! We stayed in the town of Victoria Falls, and three times ventured to the park opposite the Falls to view them. They are a marvel to behold! About a mile long and 420 feet deep, the waters of the Zambezi drop straight down on the Zambian side into a gorge about 400 feet wide, to flow out at a 90 degree angle, only to turn by another 90 degrees at the end of the gorge. Three visits were not enough – we also took a helicopter tour to view this spectacle from the air.

Below the Falls, when the river has made its two 90 degree turns, it continues rushing through another winding gorge, called The Boiling Pot. Rafting trips are offered to those brave enough to run these level 5 rapids. I had seen a couple of videos of these runs and inquired with an American river runner who had been there. What I had seen and was told, made Ute and me desist from this excitement. I was not looking forward needing to be flown from there with a serious injury to an African hospital. Our fellow travelers dared it, and flipped their raft in one of the rapids. Unable to right it before the next rapids, they hung on for dear life. Christa and Debby thought that their last minute had come!

To Ute and me the repeated sight of the natural wonder of Moise-oa-Tunya sufficed and became a fitting experience before our departure from this, today, so troubled land.

Moroccan Impressions

In March of 2001, together with a couple of friends, I traveled through Morocco with O.A.T., Overseas Adventure Travel. For personal reasons my wife, Ute, had decided to cancel her participation shortly before departure, but had always remained interested in experiencing Morocco and its cuisine.

So, in April of 2010, together with another couple of friends, Matt and Roseann, whom we had met on an earlier trip through New Zealand, we ventured off again with the same organization for a repeat of my earlier trip.

Royal Air Maroc took us to Casablanca, where we were met at the airport by our trip leader, Aziz Kebiri, wearing the customary jallabiyy, a frock-like garment. A faint memory of his name and appearance triggered a series of questions: "Did you, or do you live in Fez?" "Yes". "Do you have a daughter 13 or 14 years old?" "Yes." "Do you have a BA in English literature?" "Yes."

Then we hugged! Of all ten of O.A.T.'s Morocco guides, I had 'found' Aziz once more! *Kebir,* also spelled *Kabir,* in Arabic means 'large;' *al-akbar* is its superlative, the 'greatest.' This is what I called Aziz by trip's end: Aziz al-akbar!

He continued saying: "I have now two more children." Knowing that he leads ten tours each year, and takes another three exploratory trips to scout out new places to go to for 14 years now, I asked: "How do you get more children?" "By cell phone," came the response. And, yes, he was using an iPhone – but only for making trip arrangements. And mobile phones were everywhere. I saw a shepherd with his flock in the field using a phone.

Morocco is a country in transition, in social matters as well as public works works. One finds women covered in veils, and in the cities women dressed like anywhere else in the West. And teaching the young has great priority. The young Moroccan king Mohammed VI, has married a commoner with a Ph.D. in computer science. A picture of the king can be found in all public buildings, but I noticed at least six different images; on two of them he even looked pensive. This is very much different from dictatorships, where the head honcho's image is always the same, looking more or less sternly down on his subjects. Bridge and road building goes on across the country, and Moroccans, having worked or working in European countries, invest their savings by building houses across Morocco. However, since real estate taxes need only be paid once the building is finished, most don't finish it and leave an upper floor open to the elements.

In Casablanca we viewed a magnificent mosque, designed by a Christian Frenchman. The building looks more like a church than a mosque. We walked the beach promenade, had tea at a beach-front restaurant, and stopped at Sam's Cafe of Humphrey Bogart and Ingrid Bergman fame.

Then we drove on to Rabat, Morocco's capital city. We stood before the magnificent entrance gate to the royal palace, visited the *Medina*, the old center of the city with its *Souk*, the market, and the lavish mausoleum of Mohammed V, and Mohammed II's father, Hassan II. It was designed by a Vietnamese architect. A huge mosque, its construction began in the 1200s, was never finished and most of it was destroyed in the 1755 earthquake that also leveled Lisbon. Only its 145 foot tall minaret remains standing.

At Rabat's outskirts we viewed the ruins of Chellah, known to the Romans as Sala Colonia. The Almohad dynasty used the ghost town as a necropolis. One of its leaders, Abu l-Hasan, built, among other structures, a mosque there, which include his own tomb and that of his British-born wife and daughter. These structures, too, suffered severely from the 1775 earthquake.

In a meeting room at our hotel, Aziz gave us a basic Arabic lesson. We learned, tried to remember, and later applied a few of the words, like '*Balak!*,' watch out!, "*Salam alaikum*", peace to you, and its response, "*Alaikum as-salam*". Important was *"Shukran,"* thank you, which we subsequently used liberally. And then there was "*Yallah!*," let's go, important to keep the 16 of us going. "*La*," no, was also important to get the many vendors to leave us be.

And, like the names of many stars in our northern skies, Western languages have adopted numerous terms from Arabic, like "*Sukar*", sugar, and *al-Kahul*, alcohol, telling that Islamic countries knew very well, despite the Qur'an's urgings, how to produce it, whether as beer, wine, or spirits.

And on we went to Volubilis, the ruins of an ancient Roman town, abandoned in 300 AD. It was the westernmost Roman settlement, a military and trading post, at its height housing about 20,000 people. It features some magnificent mosaics. Its ruins were further collapsed by the 1775 earthquake, centered in the Cape Verde islands in the Atlantic ocean, that destroyed Lisbon.

About 60% of Morocco's population is Berber, with a small contingent of black people from south of the Sahara. The remainder are Arabs, who entered the country after the Berbers, who may be the descendants of Visigoths, the western Goths, a Germanic tribe. The Visigoths ventured, from what is today called Central Europe to sack Rome. From there, they moved on to France and Spain where they established kingdoms, with some tribes possibly crossing the Straits of Gibraltar. Today, the Berbers are more 'liberal' Muslims than their Saudi Arab brethren, as is usually the case for people living at the periphery of a religious system. And while Westerners call these people 'Berbers,' they prefer to refer to themselves as 'Amazighs.'

The Moors, Amazighs, Saracens, as they are variously called, occupied Spain from the 8th to the 13th century, establishing there a vibrant, scholarly culture far beyond what Europe was producing at the time, with Muslims, Jews and Christians living peacefully side-by-side. After the remnant of the Moorish al-Andalus kingdom succumbed to the Christian onslaught in 1492, the attempt of the Spanish Crown to force the conversion of Jews to the Christian faith caused many of them to emigrate to Morocco and to Europe, contributing to the blossoming of the Renaissance. From the late 8th century to the 9th, the Saracens even occupied most of Provence all the way into Switzerland, providing a relatively more cultured environment than that of the surrounding Franks.

We entered Meknes, and its *Medina*, there visited the *Mellah*, the old Jewish quarter, and a still functioning synagogue. We entered the immense vaults of Moulay Ismail's granary, built by slaves, then stood before Ismail's mausoleum. He was a cruel warrior king, but is considered one of the greatest figures in Moroccan history, who made Meknes his royal city and beat the advancing Turks to a standstill. He was a contemporary of Louis XVI and tried to make Meknes the Moroccan Versailles. Ruling for 65 years, he is supposed to have fathered 889 children, 525 sons and 342 daughters, a feat that would have required a more than daily 'engagement' of his.

Meknes, and many other towns north of the Rif and Atlas mountains, are blessed by fertile soil, providing an abundance of vegetables, fruits and olives. Several rivers supply plenty of water and hydroelectric energy.

Matt and Roseann wanted to see the 'forbidden' hill town of Moulay Idriss, so Aziz took us there. It was established by Moulay Idriss I, who is buried there in a mausoleum, a major pilgrimage site. The term *Moulay* is roughly equivalent to 'Saint.' Idriss established the town in 787 AD, after he fled from the Middle East. He is the founder of the first Arabian dynasty and introduced Islam to Morocco. We walked the town to the mausoleum's entrance, which was barred at chest height by a 4x4 wooden beam, the limit of passage for non-Muslims. Imagine this at a European cathedral! And, for whatever reason, we saw a huge number of Mercedes taxis parked in town. They are called 'German Camels' in Morocco.

And then came Fez with its ancient warren of a *Medina* and *Souk*, housing about 600,000 people! Aziz, having grown up there, engaged a special guide, a very distinguished-looking man by the name of Hamad Ali, as a back-up to take us through this part of town. He was needed so that none of our group would get lost in its narrow crisscrossing alleyways, where only donkeys, mules and push carts are permitted for transportation. Here is where we liberally applied the warning "Balak!, Balak!", watch out!, watch out!, and heard it from others when huge piles of materials were transported through the alleys and everyone had to step to the walls.

We visited a store where delicate scarves are woven, worn by Tuaregs on their heads to protect their faces from the sirocco-borne sands. Except for myself, everyone of our group equipped themselves with at least one. Then, along another alleyway, steep stairs led up to a leather shop. At the entrance mint leaves were handed to us to cover up the penetrating odor of the freshly tanned leather. Having been at this store before, I must say that I've never seen as many leather items as there. From a couple of windows on the upper floor one looked down on about 30 open tanning vats in different colors – a very picturesque site. In some, workmen were trampling the hides with their feet!

Despite the many rugs we were shown at a cooperative, none of us decided to purchase one. A bit later we had lunch in the *Medina*. Before all this, outside the *Medina*, we viewed the ornate entrance to another royal palace, and visited a pottery place with ceramics galore.

168

Aziz again showed the kindness of inviting all 16 of us to his condo, a setting not too dissimilar from Western interiors, except that a large formal room had sitting benches all around with a table in its middle. He introduced us to his wife, a teacher, his children, and live-in help. Here in Fez, we split up into three smaller groups, each being hosted one evening for dinner by a local city family. In our case, the host was a school inspector who travels the surrounding area, where he inspects every teacher for proficiency at five year intervals. We had plenty of questions for him, and he some for us, but when he mentioned that his three children attend private schools, and I asked him: "How so?," he being a public school inspector, jokingly embarrassed, put a catalog in front of his face.

The French occupied Morocco from 1906 to 1956. They built some infrastructure and in many cities what are nowadays called 'new towns,' as opposed to the *Medinas*, the old towns. During their 50-year occupation they never dared enter the Fez *Medina*!

After Fez, we headed south instead of east, to and through the Middle Atlas, the Rif mountains. We stopped in Ifrane, a mountain town, where Aziz was once stranded for three days by snowfalls with an O.A.T. group. We took a walk through town, which looked like a European Alpine village. It had been a summer retreat for the French from the lowland heat, but also a ski area. And there was also another royal palace and a magnificent monument commemorating the last of the Berber lions killed there.

And on it went, this becoming the longest drive of the trip – about 300 miles. It may not sound like much, but the two-lane, often winding road limited speeds to a maximum of 50 mph, and usually less. In the hills, the road was often 'lined' with jars of honey locals were selling. By arrangement, we stopped with a semi-nomadic family who served us tea in their winter residence, a dwelling made from various materials. In summer these people take their flocks of sheep - our host owned a 'small' herd of 400, as he called it – to higher elevations. At one time, we looked down onto a narrow but giant oasis about 60 miles in length. At a lookout, Ute was approached by a little Moroccan girl with a digital camera asking her to stand next to her mother for picture taking. The evening found us nearer the Sahara, in Erfoud, in the Riad Salam (Garden of Peace) hotel, a fancy-looking, cavernous place with a nice, big swimming pool. However, the rooms and their sinks did carry a peculiar odor. A cold beer by the pool side, shared with Aziz, was a consolation.

The following day, on our way to the tent camp, we stopped at a place for an hour's prearranged camel ride across the sand dunes. Upon its conclusion, we were hosted to a good lunch in the middle of nowhere. After another short drive – from Erfoud we now traveled in four Toyota Land Cruisers – we stopped at the abode of a music and dance group, the *Gnaoua Khamlia*, the Sand Pigeons. Well, to me they truly sounded like pigeons, but then, I may not be much of a music connoisseur.

Just about all of us had stocked up on Moroccan wines in Rabat, some being very good, and most were intended to be drunk sitting around a fire the following two evenings at our tented camp at the edge of the Sahara. Well, the Sirocco was blowing. It starts in April. We spent a miserable night in our tents, the canvas flapping, with sand and dust coming in to grime our faces.

By morning the wind had lessened and we took a walk across the sandy, rocky area to some nomads' tent. In the afternoon, a cooking lesson was given in the dining tent, concentrating on the Moroccan *Tajine*, an earthenware saucer-like container with a conical hood of the same material. The *Tajine* comes in various sizes to feed one person or an entire family. First, some rice or precooked couscous is heaped in the dish's center, then chicken, beef or lamb pieces are put on top – but no pork, a no-no in the Muslim world – to be surrounded by various vegetables, like onions, tomatoes, carrots, aubergine, zucchini, etc., with some preserved lemon topping the pile. Different spices are added, like saffron, cumin, cinnamon, salt, etc. With the hood on, the vessel is then placed on hot coals or a stove top and, voilà, after about 45 minutes a delicious, tender meal is ready to be served.

Let me describe here the food we were served at various locations, whether in private homes, restaurants along the road, or in hotels. Except for some occasions, when we received a soup first – and always good bread – a salad was never missing. It came either in individual servings or on a communal plate, where each item was placed separately. It usually consisted of tomato, cucumber, potato, aubergine, carrots and red beets. This was often followed by some shish kababs, then, in turn, came a *Tajine* with either chicken, beef, or lamb and the accompanying vegetables. Oranges, apples, and bananas made up the desert, at times also cookies.

Later that afternoon, it was decided to return to the Riad Salam hotel in Erfoud, so as not to suffer another windy night in the tents. Nine years ago in March, in a nearby tent camp, we had fires in the evening, alas, no wine, and in the morning we climbed a giant sand dune to watch the sunrise. Not this year, though!

The next day saw us on the road once more, now heading west, when we passed a group of semi-monads with their donkeys loaded to the hilt with the family's entire belongings, including some chickens. Everyone had to get out of the cars and take pictures. The people were happy to accept some dirhams, the local currency, in compensation.

We were now on the way to the Todra Gorge, a potentially scenic setting. Unfortunately, the road leading through it is under construction and tourist travel is overwhelming. It was a mess. A large hotel complex in the gorge dates its beginnings to its owner once living in a cave behind today's structures and serving tea to tourists. He, supposedly, saved diligently and eventually was able to gradually build this fancy hotel. Today, in his nineties, he is supposed to live in Tinerhir.

In Tinerhir we stayed at the nice hotel Kenzi Saghro on top of a hill, from where we overlooked the town and the community's rich fields, watered by the river rushing from the gorge. On the afternoon of our arrival, some of our ladies and a couple of gents decided to try the *Hammam*, the baths, where the sexes, of course are separated. This is also where Muslims perform their major ablutions.

We walked the narrow lanes through the fields, observing how the people lived and worked. Quietly – it was difficult to get our chattering group to fall silent – we passed through overgrown fruit and olive orchards, listening to the birds and the gurgle of the water in the small irrigation channels. From there, we walked up to a *Duar*, a community settlement of adobe structures. Next to it stood the ruins of an older *Duar*, abandoned years ago, when it became too cumbersome to maintain. Thus, its occupants simply built a new, extensive settlement next to it.

Back in town, we first visited a girls vocational center, then ambled through a *Souk* and, lo and behold – a small red-light district. Continuing, we arrived at a school where boys from poor backgrounds are broadly educated. We were served lunch in their refectory, with two boys joining us at each of our tables. These boys, from 12 to 18 years of age, were very well-mannered, the older ones able to converse with us in French or English. I talked at some length with the school's director and complimented him on his accomplishments.

Later, we visited a Berber carpet store, run by a Tuareg family. Their spokesman, dressed in native garb and fluent in English, could be called a ham – jest intended – and came across as quite sophisticated. After his introductions, we were taken to a showroom – and now one beautiful rug after another was placed before our eyes, while we were served the customary mint tea, either with or without sugar. Walking into the room, I spotted a rug on a wall and, despite us having enough – I had purchased already two Berber rugs in Morocco nine years ago – I immediately fell in love with it. When I mentioned it to Ute, she had also already succumbed to its appeal. Well, what do you expect after being married for 49 years? I asked for its price and was given the equivalent of approximately $ 2,000. Knowing that, I walked over to Aziz and asked him for how much he thought I could get it for. He had earlier told us that, in most places, we could usually dicker down prices to one-third of the initially quoted price. He gave $ 800 as a target price. Well, I got it for $ 775. We had it rolled up and it later went into one of our duffles. Some other members of our group could not resist either, and we must have left the store a few thousand dollars poorer, but richer in beauty, and having enriched some Moroccan people.

In the evening, some of us ventured to a woman's place, an expert in Henna painting. Precocious Ute went first and had the inside of her right hand decorated. Being a lefty, she was able to continue feeding and washing herself the first two days, until the application had properly set. Now, two weeks later, her Henna application is slowly fading.

Leaving Tinerhir the next day, we stopped at a large house one could almost call a *Kasbah*, a citadel. Its owner had several wives and numerous children. There we were shown the baking of a 'Berber pizza.' This is a hand-flattened wheat dough upon which a small amount of various diced vegetables is piled, then wrapped in like a calcione. Then the 'pizza' was baked in a small, wood-fired oven in a very smoky room. It was delicious.

172

Heading now towards the Dada Gorge we left almost all tourists behind. Eventually, we had to switch to two smaller local buses to maneuver the winding road through this picturesque canyon.

On the return, we stopped at a large house, the home of an *Imam*, leader of prayers in the mosque. The building, with its very pleasing large room for social gatherings of the community, had been for generations in the *Imam's* family. Many rugs were spread on the floor, with seating, as usual, around its walls. A substantial audio system in one corner and an overhead projector in another, indicated the technological facilities. At a few tables at one corner, the *Imam's* brother, an *Imam*-in-training, served us lunch. An *Imam*, studying in a *Madrassa*, a school, must memorize the entire Qur'an, before he can be an *Imam*, a project of years.

After lunch we were given the opportunity to ask the *Imam* questions of whatever nature. He described also that his function was elective and as much social as religious, and that he could be voted out by the community if his performance was found wanting.

Neither of the two men spoke English, so that Aziz had to translate back and forth. The exchange, despite the sometimes incisive and not-so-incisive questions, was often interrupted by the two men's and Aziz's laughter. I could not help asking the question about the Qur'an's position on atheism, citing what Salman Rushdie, an avowed Muslim atheist, had experienced. The response of this man was, that the Qur'an frowns seriously on two 'sins:' atheism and neglecting charity to the poor. Well, depending on how one defines 'poor' these days, I might squeak through and, since an astronomer-friend has named an asteroid after me – I am already in the heavens. Among many other things, the *Imam* stated was, that Islam is a peaceful religion – that may be so – but all human enterprises – and religions are part of them – have failings. Contemporary Islam is convulsed by some of its failings, intolerant and not-so-peaceful expressions, which take more lives from among its believers than of Westerners.

After another night at the hotel, we transferred back to a bus that took us to Quarzazate to a very Western-ambiance hotel, another Riad Salam, where rock music played in the central garden around the swimming pool, next to which we had our meals buffet-style. In the afternoon, our group, minus myself,

173

were taken to a Berber museum and a *Duar*, whose tight-knit community, marrying only within, showed effects of inbreeding.

In the morning, off again, we stopped at a substantial ancient *Kasbah*, named Kar of Aitbenhadou, the site where many movies were shot, among them 'Lawrence of Arabia.' Driving through the High Atlas, we saw its highest peak, Mount Toubkal, rising to 13,671 ft. It was a very scenic, also very winding drive. Marrakech now lay just ahead, which we reached that afternoon.

Ah, Marrakech! Its history, its allure, its lively life! Once, it was the end point of the salt caravans, bringing rock salt from south of the Sahara, then worth its weight in gold. We were accommodated at the Hotel el-Andalous, the best of all the hotels we had stayed in, except that its buffet-style food was geared to the taste of the many French visitors, with few, if any, Moroccan items. It is just too much to describe all of Marrakech's sites in detail. An early morning buggy ride took us into town, where we viewed the Koutoubia minaret, the Saadian tombs, the Bahia palace, then entered the Moorish spice market and a Berber pharmacy. A beautiful garden, Jardin Majorelle, with a profusion of subtropical plants and trees, and gorgeous bougainvillea, was restored and is now maintained by the Yves Saint Laurent estate. The garden also holds the dispersed ashes of the fashion designer. We also visited the well-adorned premises of an old *Madrassa*, where young boys once spent years of their lives memorizing the Qur'an, an arduous task that, if and when it had been accomplished, opened up various 'careers' in public life. Their cells looked down onto the central court, where a large running-water basin was available for their minor ablutions prior to prayer: the washing of face, hands and feet.

And then there was the *Medina* with its central open plaza, the Djemma el-Fna Square, where, during the day, some merchants and snake charmers, shaded by umbrellas, ply their trade. At night, this plaza turns into a magical place and, with its packed food stalls, becomes a meeting place of the world, where one can eat cheaply some exotic dishes, like sheep's heads, escargot, and whatnot. The food smells can be overwhelming, just as are the crowds of people. We did not dine there, but retired to the Dar Essalam restaurant, the Abode of Peace, as part of our 'Mysterious Morocco' tour. Its splendid Salon Marjane became fully occupied and we enjoyed, along with red and white Moroccan wines, some delicious local foods. A female dancer,

174

balancing a tablet with several burning candles on her head, made her way from a central dance area along the tables. She was followed by an attractive belly dancer, who did likewise, also to collect the guests contributions for her performance. Jerry, one of our tour participants, performed some gyrations with her.

The evening concluded our common tour and ten participants left for home. Now, three couples, Matt & Roseann, Paul & Barbara, and Ute & I, were ready for our post-trip. A small bus, and, of course Aziz, took us to the Cascades d'Ouzoud, a most beautiful, high waterfall some distance outside Marrakech, where we had our open-air lunch in full sight of the falls. The path down to the restaurant and falls was lined with the stalls of merchants, hawking their wares. Ute was 'hawked' by a couple of items.

On the way to the falls, Aziz spotted a market taking place in a small village and had our driver stop to visit this *Souk,* where farmers sold their produce and where just about everything else could be bought. Following his advice, we left all valuables in our bus, then walked the crowded lanes between the stalls. At one point, when Aziz talked with two of the merchants standing before us, Ute asked whether she could take their picture. They readily agreed, and Ute, thinking that she owed them a couple of dirhams, offered them to the two men. But they smiled, one waved his hand, reached into his pocket, and handed Ute two dirhams. It so happened that to the left of the two men stood a young woman, her palm outstretched for a handout, which now was quick in coming – the same two dirhams passing into her hand!

Instead of being on our own the following day, we made special arrangements with Aziz for a ride to the Atlantic coast town of Essaouira, in the 1960s a hippie hangout. We stopped at a Women's Cooperative along the road where they produce Argan oil from a tree nut. This very fine oil is used for cosmetic, medical, and cooking purposes. The establishments' facilities ranged from very modern, the acceptance of credit cards, to primitive, where five woman were cracking the nuts with stone tools, then one grinding the mush to oil on a hand-turned stone mill – but it kept them in work.

Aziz had told us earlier that in the traditional Berber communities, women, once married, were expected to bear children as soon as possible. If, after two years no offspring was produced, they were often divorced. They were then without support and could find it only by marrying an older, widowed man.

It became a long drive, and when we arrived in Essaouira, a very strong wind was blowing in from the ocean, making walking along the shore and ancient fortifications not very pleasant. We took refuge in its *Medina*, where, among other stores, we visited one specializing in wood inlays using the root of a special tree. The work shown was exquisite in its detail and fit. It was much better than the ceramic and filigree work we had seen everywhere, which, at close distance can look rough, gaining its ornamental magnificence only from a distance.

There was one more day left. Another bus ride took us into the mountain villages of Ouirgane and Asni. Before we had lunch at our host's home, Ali, a guard at a nearby resort owned by a Frenchman, we rode off on a 45-minute mule ride, uphill along a narrow, winding, and very much overgrown trail which, for some distance, was also the bed of a small brook. It was fun, though, and our steeds were well-behaved.

It was a 'packed' trip with memorable experiences, especially those where we were able to meet the always friendly people. The next morning Royal Air Maroc took us from Marrakech to Casablanca and from there back to New York.

Galápagos

January 9-19, 2007

When in 1535 Bishop Tomás de Berlanga's galleon, on a trip from Panama to Peru was blown off course, its crew discovered the Galápagos Isles, about 1,000 km to the west of the coast of Ecuador. The bishop described the giant turtles found there from which the islands received their name.

The islands became a favorite hangout for buccaneers and, later, visiting whalers, who, it is estimated, took more than 100,000 turtles from there, stacking them alive in their holds as fresh meat supplies.

Then, in 1835, Charles Darwin visited on the Beagle, observing those turtles, also eating them, as well as taking recordings of geology, botany, land and marine animals and those famous finches – except that he didn't record from which island they came! Anyway, those finches played only a subsidiary role in his Theory of Evolution.

12 main islands plus 12 minor ones, all volcanic, are the product of a hot spot similar to Hawaii and Reunion, the oldest island being about five million years old. Basaltic lava flows from various shield volcanoes continue to erupt, giving all islands a very rough terrain.

My wife Ute and I had booked our trip with Wilderness Travel, flying into Quito, Ecuador's capital, at 2,500 m elevation. A tour took us through its Old Town, a World Heritage Site, its many churches, and the presidential palace. It all concluded with a sumptuous dinner at a Spanish restaurant with lots of tapas and Spanish wine. The dinner was to be a seafood casserole or paella. Precocious me, I jested with our host whether I could come back the next day for paella, having the seafood casserole tonight. Well, courteous as our hosts were, I got both. The following day an Airbus A320 took us to Isla Baltra, Galápagos' main airport. In WW2 Baltra housed a US military base for the defense of the Panama Canal. Today 97% of the islands are national park, which can be visited only with a guide.

Though eons the creatures native to the islands flew or rafted there from the mainland. Seeds carried on the feet or in the stomachs of wayward birds vegetated the once utterly barren grounds. The marine iguanas, unique to Galápagos, once land

177

animals, had to sustain themselves on seaweed, in order to survive upon arrival, thus evolving in this manner.

We boarded the brigantine Diamante with the other 10 passengers and our knowledgeable and caring guide Fausto Arellano, then skippered over to the north shore of Seymour island. On our first land excursion we walked past frigate birds, the males expanding their big, flaming-red throat pouches, waiting for females flying overhead to descend and chose them for mating. We saw our first blue-footed boobies doing their funny mating rituals, lifting first one foot then the other, then stretching and raising their heads in unison. Their name is derived from the Spanish word 'bobo', meaning clown, a true application of the term. Later on we took our first snorkel excursion in calm waters, seeing a variety of tropical fishes, among which were barracudas and sharks. My most pleasing experience was a little 2" black-striped fish, which 'attached' itself to me for the entire range, dashing about in front of me, sometimes only 10 cm from my mask.

All in all we visited nine islands, small and large. The distances between them were usually covered by night, so that we had the following day available for land and marine excursions. This meant that engine noise and the sometimes substantial wallowing of our ship rocked us to sleep. Never did we need to partake of our supply of Dramamine, although Ute liberally dispensed it to some of our fellow passengers.

The next morning saw us at Santa Fé island. Upon landing we spotted a Galápagos hawk perched on a stone marker. Everyone took close-up pictures of the utterly unafraid being. Then we walked past sea lions, land iguanas, boobies and frigate birds. Giant cactus trees spread along most of our walkway. In the afternoon we arrived at Academy Bay on Santa Cruz island with its main town of Puerto Ayora. A walk there took us to the Darwin research station, where, among land iguanas and turtles, we got a glimpse of Lonesome George, a desk-size tortoise, the last of his species from one of the islands. The station is engaged in breeding tortoises and land iguanas for repopulating of several islands, where stocks have been severely depleted due to introduced foreign creatures and pests. These days the total number of human inhabitants on all the islands is about 20,000 ;-).

A long and bumpy overnight trip took us south to Isla Española and plenty of nasca   and blue-footed boobies, albatross and marine iguanas along a rather hot walk. Really – the tameness of the animals is something to behold! If one wanted to – it's not allowed – one could pet many of them. At the end of the hike a small lighthouse provided the only shade far and wide until our pickup by the dinghy.

The next day found us at Isla Floreana at Punta Cormorant and the Devil's Crown, the 10-12 m tall broken basaltic remnants of a marine crater. Five intrepid explorers ventured out to snorkel the broken remains in an S-curve in rather rough waters. Sure, there was interesting marine life, however – I, a poor swimmer with only first-time experience using flippers, became quickly overcome by the experience and had to make an effort returning to the accompanying dinghy to get out of the water. My only comfort was, that two others had to do the same some time later.

By afternoon we anchored in Post Office Bay, a relic from whaling times, when whalers were away from home for years at a time. It became a custom to leave letters in something akin to a mail box for people of returning ships to leave through the deposited letter addresses to carry to the folks back home. Today tourists can leave their stamp-less postcards for other visitors coming through to carry to their destinations. Ute picked up two; one for Scottsdale and one for Tucson. I had one card destined for Tasmania and didn't dare put it in the box for fear it wouldn't arrive in the lifetime of the recipient. After another long overnight sail we found ourselves at Punta Moreno on the biggest island of the archipelago, Isla Isabela. A major lava flow had covered the area all the way to the ocean. I must mention here, that access to the land is permitted only at designated spots where white-tipped stakes mark the route a group of tourists may take. Following these, we passed by several lower-level ponds of brackish water, but with rather lush vegetation in the otherwise barren landscape. They were home to ducks and flamingos.

Ute and I helped our lone Argentine couple to negotiate the treacherous terrain. I felt, by myself, I could have been "rock flying", as Johanna Angermeyer called it in a chapter of her book, *"My Father's Island"*, the story of five brothers leaving Germany upon the rise of the Nazis, journeying to Galápagos to make their life there. I read Johanna's book from the ship's library. Today, some of the Angermeyer's descendants own several brigantines, the Diamante, the somewhat larger Sagitta, and others.

179

In the afternoon a short sail took us to Elizabeth Bay. In our dinghy we entered several narrow mangrove-framed arms where the outboard motor was shut off and, in silence, we were propelled forward only by oar strokes. This made it possible to spot a number of big green sea turtles and a hawksbill in this retreat. Then Fausto pointed out several "tree lions", actually sea lions, which had climbed up fallen, now inclined tree trunks, taking their snooze up there. That evening the clouds broke and we experienced a beautiful sunset, later on seeing Orion at the zenith.

Isabela originally consisted of six separate islands, each formed by its own volcano. A narrow isthmus at Elizabeth Bay is covered by a major, very rugged lava bed. Once Isabela was home to close to 100,000 feral goats, their ancestry going back to goats being set out on the islands by buccaneers as fresh meat supplies, and multiplied escapees from the farms on southern Isabela. Since they severely affected the native wildlife and vegetation, a program was developed to eradicate the herds, at least on the northern part of Isabela, the lava-covered isthmus providing an impenetrable barrier between south and north Isabela. The cost estimate was one million dollars. New Zealand sharpshooters with helicopters were brought in who eradicated the northern herds to the last animal, the corpses rotting away, providing food for various flesh eaters. Today, the land is still littered with the bleached bones of goats. When the program was finished it had run up to costing 20 million dollars!

A short overnight ride took us to Bahia Urbina on Isabela, where we did a morning hike through the brush area, seeing plenty of big land iguanas, all of which numbered for observation. Right at the beginning of our hike a huge tortoise came ambling down our trail providing for a great photo opportunity. With sandy beach areas for egg laying in short supply, these tortoises, as well as the land iguanas, climb all the way up the flanks of the volcano, then descend inside to find loose material in which to deposit their clutch of eggs. Then the newborn have to make their arduous walk back down into areas where they can find food. The hike led us through a section of desiccated logs and branches, remnants of a once flourishing mangrove forest, in the 1950s uplifted five meters by an earthquake.

A short sail across Canal Bolivar brought us to Punta Espinosa on Fernandia Island, where I decided to let everyone see more marine iguanas and birds, whereas I spent the solitude on deck reading. I figured, being the oldest of our group, yet, maybe, still one of the nimblest on land, I deserved to take my leave whenever I felt like it. I had just finished reading Kurt Vonnegut's satirical and pessimistic novel *Galápagos* from the ship's library, in which he describes humanity's devolution. But he also described how marine iguanas, feeding on seaweed at low tide, with males diving up to 10 m to feed and staying up to five minutes under water, line themselves up afterwards on the rocks to have the sun 'cook' their food. My returning wife confirmed the lineup of iguanas doing just that.

Then we took off under sail to round the northern tip of Isabela with everyone assembled on the bow of the Diamante, drinking wine and watching whales surfacing and, eventually, experience another gorgeous sunset, the Sagitta paralleling us in the distance.

By morning we had arrived at Punta Egas on Isla San Salvadore, where I decided on one more snorkel adventure among a wide-spaced lava outcropping, our dinghy anchored in the middle. The water was not very deep and a variety of fishes could be seen, however the back and forth surges of the waters once more became too much for me and, unpleasantly, the dinghy was nowhere to be seen, hidden by one of the outcroppings. Well, I made it back to the boat, but decided that this had been my last snorkel in open waters. A hike along the broken lava-covered shore with many partially inundated lava tubes, took us past sea lions and a small colony of fur seals. The ubiquitous bright-red sally lightfoot crabs scampered about wherever we landed.

Cruising along Salvadore's north shore we arrived at the small island of Bartolomé where a few of us, despite the rain, climbed the 300 plus stairs up Pinnacle Rock, remnant of an extinct volcano. That evening our cook prepared a sumptuous farewell repast in his tiny kitchen which we took in the inside cabin/dining room due to inclement weather – the rainy season had begun. Aside from our captain, Ernesto, our crew consisted of the cook, a mechanic, a sailor and a stewart with overlapping duties. Everyone was always helpful and courteous. Often, though, we had taken breakfast, lunches, and dinners on a nicely arranged outside table, a tarp protecting us at daytime from the tropical sun.

Very early next morning another dinghy ride took us into a mangrove bay at Coleta Tortuga Negra on Isla Santa Cruz, however few siting were made on this last venture. Then it was back to Isla Baltra to catch our plane back to Quito. That evening we enjoyed another farewell dinner outside town with tapas and Argentine steak.

After this our group parted, some returning home, others venturing farther. We visited the anthropological museum in the morning, once more the flee market and a spiffy gallery to pick up some souvenirs. The Hilton Colon was nice enough to let us stay in our room until 20:00 after which we were taken by our city guide William to the airport for the night flight home to Phoenix via Atlanta.

The Galápagos Islands are justifiably famous for the tameness, peculiarity and variety of their wildlife nowhere else to be found on the planet. To our guide I called them at one time: The Serengeti of the Pacific. But, like everywhere else, it is a 'paradise', an environment compromised, which, to restore, a number of organizations are working on very hard. Its lands are still raw and, because of the still erupting volcanoes will remain raw for times to come. The vegetation, being limited in variety, is unattractive. But in the rawness of the land and how life took a foothold, even prospered, lies their attractiveness.

Alaska

The last Terrestrial Frontier of the US

September 18, 2006

In three hops Alaska Airlines took us from Phoenix via Seattle and Anchorage to Fairbanks. On the leg from Anchorage to Fairbanks we even got to see the top of Mount McKinley, largest mountain in the USA with 20,320 ft, rising white above a solid cloud deck.

The next day our tour with Cruise West took us on a two hour trip on a sternwheeler along the Chena River at Fairbanks to its confluence with the larger Tanana River, which carried a heavy load of silt, rock flour from the glaciers farther south, producing a wild swirl of mixing waters. Along the Chena people built their homes. The recent governor Murkowski's wife came to its banks to greet our passing ship; a bit farther downstream Susan Butcher's husband, she the winner of the Iditarod Race, who had just died from Leukemia, came to the water with his son and dog caretakers to wave to us and talk with the boat's owner, all giving the impression of down-homeness in this still raw land, more than twice the area of Texas.

And, as the story was told us: Years ago when Pope John Paul happened to pass through Fairbanks and President Reagan was also in town, the two met at the then senator Murkowski's house and, that the heavy, armored president's car sunk into the senator's unpaved driveway and had to be extracted. The oil spill from BP's pipe line from Prudhoe Bay was all the talk at the time. It turned out that BP had not send a scanning device through the pipe for years to check for erosion, when, for instance, the transalpine pipe from Italy to Germany is checked monthly! Yet, every Alaskan resident, man, woman and child, can expect this year to receive a tax handout of about $1,000 from oil revenues. And – there's no income tax in the state.

Today, Alaska has a population of 650,000, spread over a land area of 570,000   square miles. The US purchased it from Russia in 1867 for 7.2 million in gold, representing 1.67 billion in 2006 dollars. Cheap! Yet, at the time some called it "Seward's Folly", Seward, who had promoted the purchase, then being Secretary of State.

183

The following day bus ride took us to Denali National Park and, subsequently, another bus deep into the Park. Denali provided a glimpse of the grandeur of this harsh land, with its broad expanses and, as it appears, plentiful tree and growth cover. However we learned that the annual rainfall in the interior is only 12 inches on average per year, less than the Southwest gets. Rain clouds are kept from the interior by the northern Brooks Mountain Range and the southern Alaska Range. The difference to the Southwest deserts is the muskeg, the boggy ground, which traps the moisture, thus providing for more luxuriant growth. Except for a moose and some caribou we did not get to see any wildlife; Mt. McKinley also barely showed its base below the clouds.

That evening we had opted for a Heli-hike tour. A helicopter took us, together with another couple and a naturalist guide up to alpine tundra for a four hour hike across soggy grounds on which over one hundred different plant species grow, among them willow trees only a few inches tall. The five mile walk was a delight! Up and down we went, our guide staying in radio touch with the helicopter people. Eventually we were picked up at a different location by our young female pilot who, lo and behold, had received her pilot's license in our home town of Prescott, AZ.

The next morning we cruised the Nenana river in an oar-powered rubber raft, piloted by a twenty six year old woman. Prior to takeoff we were bundled up in dry-suits. I asked one of our guides: And where's the relief valve? Out-a-luck for two hours plus! However, we had the excitement of the day, when, at a bend in the river, we spotted a grizzly putzing around on the shore. Seeing us, he stood up and raised a paw twice, waving at us, it seemed. We told our guide after passing that the puppet could now be removed.

The next day the McKinley Explorer provided a wonderful train ride in a dome car from Denali to Talkeetna north of Anchorage. There a bus brought us the rest of the distance to the big city. A visit to the Native Heritage Center the next morning gave insight into the lives of some of the native people, or First Nation People, as they are nowadays called. It was interesting to learn that at the turn of the previous century some Saami families together with their reindeer herds, domesticated caribou, were brought from Finland all the way to Alaska to provide and to teach the Athabascan natives the herding of these animals for sustenance. It was a ringing success. Saami still dwell in Alaska today.

In mid-August there were only two and one half hours of darkness and, unfortunately, no coronal mass ejection directed towards Earth during our stay to let us experience the Corona Borealis, the Northern Lights.

During WWII when a Japanese attack on Anchorage was feared – the two westernmost Aleutian Islands had been occupied by the enemy – a secret military base, Whittier, was established in Prince William Sound, accessible only through a long but speedily dug tunnel across the neck of the Kenai Peninsula.

A bus took us there where we boarded our cruise ship, the Spirit of Oceanus, flagship of Cruise West. It accommodated one hundred twenty passenger. The crew was international, the Captain British, the first and second officers Russian and Ukrainian, the crew Jamaican and Filipino, with even a sprinkling of Americans, the naturalists et al.

There was Alastair Newton, an Englishman and biologist, who also ran the 'show', organizing our outings and get-togethers .

Meriwether Gill, a distant relative of Meriwether Louis & William Clark fame, a specialist in cetology, the study of whales.

Professor of Geography, Susan Hardwick, specializing in the Russian history of Alaska. A most vivacious and engaged lady.

Nancy Lord, writer an fisher-woman of many years on the Alaska coast and, last not least, the inimitable, only thirty four year old, story teller, writer and teacher, Jack Dalton, his mother native Yu'pik, his father German-American. In word and gesture he conveyed to us in several performances Yu'pik myths, particularly the Raven Creation Myth, which has spread throughout Alaska. It has experienced variations of its content, yet always retaining the Raven as the Creator and Bringer of light and life to Earth. When he had finished the Raven story and the applause had subsided, I, sitting in the front row, got up, approached him and, telling him that his presentation called for more than applause, gave him a big hug.

Stowed at the stern our ship carried five Zodiak motorized inflatables. At multiple occasions of our trip south through the Inside Passage, when farther penetration of our ship was not possible or advisable, these Zodiaks were launched by

185

crane, and eight to ten people boarded each for closer exploration of the surroundings, all piloted by the above naturalists.

On the first day of our cruise we navigated Prince William Sound, which has the most tidewater glaciers, that is a glacier reaching the sea, in Alaska. Many of these tidewater glaciers extend several tenths of feet below the water surface. Waterfalls dropped from steep cliffs on which kittiwakes nested in the hundreds. I skipped the first Zodiak excursion because – it was just too rainy, cold and miserable at the time. This is also the place of the Exxon Valdez oil spill in 1989.

The overnight passage from Prince William Sound brought us next day to Yakutat Bay with the 6 miles wide Hubbard tidewater glacier at its end. There the Zodiaks were launched for a closer approach to the calving glacier. Amazingly one part of this glacier is almost black from the rock debris it carries along, spilling icebergs, berger-bits, growlers and brash ice, as the floating ice is called in descending order of size, into the sea, adding nutrients and minerals to the Earth's oceans, a process still continuing for eons. Seals, with their cute faces, peered at us from the water or rested on the floating ice.

From Prince William Sound south to Sitka on Baranof Island the cruise crosses open water and, our ship was rolling just a bit that first night. While it made for good sleeping being gently rocked to sleep, this first dinner was not the most enjoyable for me. I did not even finish my wine when I excused myself from the table, but when I asked my wife Ute the next day how she had fared herself, she said: I did fine. I even finished your wine.

Being early risers we had breakfast 'outside', yes, outside on deck, where one could have it earlier than in the dining room. Seating for lunch and dinner was as one walked in. Tables seated from two to eight, except if one asked to be seated at a particular table. Most of the time we gathered among eight and, at times, had some lively conversations. But we also became closer to some couples and thus had dinner just the four of us. While the passengers were mostly American, there were a number of Australians and Britons, a few Germans and New Zealanders. We happened to socialize mostly with the more boisterous Aussies but also the more reserved Britons. Our favorite couples were Tony and Kerrie Jordan from Sidney and

Valerie and David Moss, originally from England, now residing in California. Who knows, we may yet see them again.

Another overnight cruise through open waters landed us next morning in Sitka. We had booked for a fishing excursion of four hours, which meant we didn't see anything of town, since the ship was to leave already shortly after noon. So, off we went on a small boat, an hour's ride into open waters with lots of bounce, to reach the fishing grounds. My first catch, hard to reel in, turned out to be a Ling cod of 45" and just as many pounds, the first fish of my life I wished to have been smaller for – it was over the legal limit. The critter had even a foot long rock bass in its mouth which I had hooked first, the cod going after it. Believe me, this is no fish story. In the really only two hour fishing time I could only land a Silver salmon, or Coho, as this species is also called, and a substantial-size rock bass.

North of Sitka lies Letuya Bay where, in 1954 an earthquake triggered an enormous rock slide at the end of the bay, causing a record tsunami with a height of 1,740 feet. Yes! 1,740 feet! Due to its remoteness 'only' a few lives were lost. A fishing boat, crewed by father and son, who survived the catastrophe, could even tell their horrific experience.

That afternoon Prof. Susan Hardwick gave a lecture on "Sitka: The Russian American Capital". And next afternoon Nancy, again, talked about "John Muir's Alaska". More lectures were usually given in the evening after dinner.

And then we arrived at Glacier Bay National Park, having now entered the Inside Passage. In the two hundred years since its discovery by Captain Vancouver the bay has become virtually ice-free. We boarded a smaller vessel, a catamaran, to penetrate deep into the fjord to better view its glaciers and wildlife, among which were Steller sea lions, even some wolves along a shoreline, all under the auspices of a park ranger and a native Tlingit, explaining his tribal background.

The Tlingit occupy a larger stretch of the Alaskan coast rich in fish and other sea life, thus their livelihood was generally insured and, as Jack Dalton explained, they had plenty of idle time to develop elaborate rituals. Somewhat in jest, he told that, when a visitor showed up, it took him half an hour to do his greetings, then the host needed another half hour to do his part. This contrasted sharply with his own tribe, the Yu'pik whose first question when a visitor arrived was: Are you hungry? Only when he was sated were greetings exchanged and other questions raised.

Skagway is a favorite port for big cruise ships, easily accommodating four to five, never mind their many thousands of passengers swamping the small town of 800 summer residents. During our presence four other such ships were in port, one of them even blocking our ship from departure at the desired time. Passengers and crew of our Spirit of Oceanus looked somewhat snobbishly with disdain on these big ships. There floated even a rumor on ours, that one of the biggies had 1,400 passengers quarantined because of an intestinal illness. Hygiene on the Oceanus was enforced by urging all passengers to was hands before eating. When entering the dining room, disinfectant wipes were handed out.

After our enjoyable four hour rail tour to the White Pass, scratching the Canadian Yukon, I remained on board of our ship, letting the hordes of big-ship tourists have Skagway. In the evening Meriwether Gill told us about Humpback whales, her specialty.

The next morning we entered Tracy Arm, a steep-sided 25 mile long fjord, eventually boarding the Zodiaks to get closer to the Dawes glacier. From here we made our way through Frederick Sound. And then – our ship was almost surrounded by what may have been fifty humpback whales doing their dives, even breaching. When the Zodiaks were launched one came diving even so close to one that it splashed its occupants, eliciting a subsequently censored exclamation of Meriwether's, the Zodiak's pilot.

On it went through the very narrow Wrangell Narrows to Petersburg on Mitkof Island where, the next day we got an introduction to the muskeg and a folk dance of the Norwegian descendants. Proliferating in the muskeg, is sphagnum moss, which can absorb thirty times its volume in water. Together with its antibacterial characteristic the British used it in WWI as a blood-absorbent. Made rich by fishing, this community looks very prosperous. Our local guide told us that her fisherman-husband paid 100,000 dollars for his lifetime halibut fishing license. Then, when last fishing for halibut was open, he caught his limit of 25,000 pounds in seven days. That afternoon Jack Dalton gave us his memorable presentation of: Raven and the Box of Light.

Down the Clarence Strait and past Ketchikan we made our way to Metlakatla on Annette Island. There, a group of

Tshimshian Indians settled in the late 1800rds after a fallout with the Canadian government, led by a dictatorial preacher. It is Alaska's only reservation. An elaborate native dance was performed in their longhouse for us tourists in. A variety of local handicraft and art objects were available.

On it went into Misty Fjords National Monument, richly deserving its name. Typical for the many Alaskan fjords is their cloudiness, although there's supposed to occur the occasional sunshine. A variety of low, wispy, long-stretched-out clouds are special. Our naturalists called them: Dragon's Breath, a poetic and well deserved name. Two rangers, one of them a woman, came in kayaks to our ship. Then we left Alaskan waters to arrive at Prince Rupert in Canada, renowned for its Salmon and Halibut fishing and canning industry. The Tshimshian Indians who had stayed put there gave us also a performance of their creation myth in their longhouse decked in their elaborate costumes. That afternoon Meriwether told about Killer Whales, or Orcas, as they ought to be called nowadays, for we do not call lions killer cats! They all have to make a living. There's also no record of an orca ever having attacked a human. Later that evening, no desert was for once offered after dinner, the ship's cooks provided a bounty of what they called the Chocoholics Gala Buffet. It was enormous!

An then the sun came out! Cruising down BC's Inside Passage, also called the Sunshine Coast, we spotted dolphins and porpoises several times, even some orcas passing along the shoreline. Sailing down some very narrow channels we eventually entered the Strait of Georgia to arrive at our destination, the port of Vancouver at 8:30 AM.

We settled into our B & B and went for a walk through what remained nearby of an Old Growth Forest park. The next morning the newly inaugurated Whistler Mountaineer took us on an all-day rail trip, which included a splendid breakfast and afternoon tea, to the alpine resort of Whistler, where the 2010 Winter Olympics are to be held.

The final day brought us to the Museum of Anthropology, affiliated with the University of British Columbia, with its excellent collection of northwest coast native art. The most impressive sculpture of over eight foot height by the Haida artist Bill Reid was The Raven and the First Men, depicting his tribe's myth, its creation story, in which the Raven, creator and simultaneously trickster finds a huge clam on the beach after the world ocean had receded and coaxed the terrified little humans out to settle the Earth.

The Myth of the Raven occurs in various permutations with the many Alaskan tribes bringing light to the world by creating the Sun, the Moon and the stars. Now – if he could once more give us the power of the Sun, the Moon, the planets and even the stars.

Monumental Sights

in Grand Staircase/Escalante, Utah, & northern Arizona.

At the end of April 2008 our group of ten, including our two guides (Nigel, a friend of mine, and his associate, Pete) drove us in two sturdy SUVs north on Hwy 89 from Prescott, AZ, to Page, by Lake Powell. Continuing on 89 toward Kanab, UT, we soon branched off north again, onto a 50 mile long gravel road through Cottonwood Canyon, along the Paria River, a few generations ago a major thoroughfare for traveling Mormons.

A little side trip on a breakneck dirt road took us to an overlook of the fantastically colored rock formations along part of this canyon valley, called Cockscomb because of its tilted strata with an undulating top. Then, a short walk on the main road's left side and we entered a most interesting slot canyon, one could easily miss, not knowing it was there – which I did on an earlier trip without a guide! Close to the road's end, we veered east for a mile to view Grosvenor Arch. At last, we arrived in the small town of Escalante, where we stayed in a motel for three nights. And why not – enjoy the comforts of life together with the sights!

Now, before getting to these sights the next day, we had to eat – and drink, the latter, concerning certain libations, being at times difficult in the State of Utah! Well, there was the 'Cowboy Blues', the only restaurant in town where we could find both good food and alcoholic drinks. And behold, from a brewery in Salt Lake City, the place had available what was branded "Polygamy Porter', it's label depicting a man surrounded by several women with a small inscription below reading: 'Why have only one'. So much for tolerance!

We were now in Escalante country. One of Bill Clinton's last act as president was to declare the Escalante area a National Monument, and it was well worth it. It is now called 'Grand Staircase/Escalante', the staircase alluding to some of its 'stepped' rock formations.

A longish drive brought us to the trail head to Spooky Gulch. Scrambling down red slick rock (sandstone) and plodding through sandy washes, we arrived at Spooky. And spooky it was! This slot canyon became ever 'slottier' as one penetrated, until I found my torso squeezed front and back. Having some slight claustrophobia, I decided to discontinue with further exploration, since I didn't care to become stuck, only to be washed out by the next flash-flood. Our other nine intrepid explorers made it through, with a couple of the men having their shirt and pant's pocket ripped – I still don't understand how some of the women made it. Maybe, it should be noted that, with the exception of Kirsten, Ed and Pete, everyone else was in excess of 65 years old.

Well, I ambled back to another interesting rock formation, a gulch called Peekaboo, which one must ascent almost vertically for about 15 feet with few hand holds. Anyway, there was a little shade from which I now observed other arrivals' attempts at getting up this cliff face. Not many did. Then a group of about 12 not-that-young-anymore-folks showed up. They spoke German. Just the other day, I had told our group, with all these Europeans clambering about in Escalante, never to call any German-speaking folks 'German', with quite a few of them being Swiss and Austrian – somehow they don't care for that. Anyway, I forgot and was quickly corrected; they were Austrian. But you ought to have seen these characters: ten of them climbed Peekaboo like a herd of mountain goats – must be in their genes coming from Austria.

After Spooky and Peekaboo – wonderful names these – we headed along 'Hole-in-the-Rock-Road to see some (more than 6,000 year old) Dinosaur tracks on top of huge slick-rock formations, white sandstone this time. To get there, we had to pass plenty of sandy gullies complete filled with huge tumbleweeds, fortunately, none needed to be crossed.

Then came Devil's Garden to walk through, following another drive to get there. These wonderfully shaped, multihued sandstone formations are the remains of an eroded plateau. Three columnar sentries guard its entrance. The views from there and many other nearby places are truly stunning!

Our congenial group survived another evening at the Cowboy Blues. Several of us were either friends, relatives, or knew each other from a previous trip; there was my wife Ute, our daughter Kirsten, friends Zene, Vern and Kathee, as well as Ed and Flo, the latter being a very down-to-earth Mormon descendent of old John D. Lee of famous Lee's Ferry at the Colorado River.

Then, by next morning we drove out to the trail head to Lower Calf Creek Falls for a six mile back-and-forth hike through a box canyon with the beautiful falls at its very end. It received its name, Calf Creek, by Mormons who fenced off the upper end of the box canyon to raise their calves in this then well protected and watered enclosure. Its vertical cliffs with their desert varnish, a group of large Indian pictographs in the distance on one of the sandstone walls across the creek and the rich vegetation of this canyon truly made it a sanctuary in this otherwise harsh, but oh so beautiful land! The most pleasant falls, ever changing and glistening in their about 126 foot tumble make for a cool environment, but I wondered whether the plunge pool is deep enough for a swim. Its outflow, Calf Creek, burbling toward the Escalante River, is full of trout. At the trail head's campsite we munched our usual lunch consisting of Subway submarines; ah well, for three days and with so much beauty, one can survive on them – and evenings there was the Cowboy Blues!

Eating there next to us every evening, was a German couple – truly – we met three times at the places we visited up there, which tells you – . He told me that, for a year, he had tried to obtain two permits from Germany via the Internet to get to The Wave at Coyote Buttes in northern Arizona; eventually, he had succeeded. Later in the year we were to also go there, as described below.

But that afternoon, after the Calf Creek walk, we drove yet Hell's Backbone Road right next to the Death Hollow Wilderness area, an about 50 mile long gravel road looping from Hwy 12 to an elevation of 8,000 ft to a lake still partly covered by ice and snow. Way up in the mountains, the road crosses a deep chasm of about 30 feet width. Nowadays, a modern concrete bridge crosses it, but it brought back memories. Once, about 14 years ago, when my wife and I drove this road and I, driving, arrived at its old rickety span of wood. I stopped and seriously considered driving back, not crossing it – that rickety it looked. But I gathered my courage and did!

While the ten of us were scrambling around this sight, I noticed that our daughter Kirsten had climbed a small rock tower right next to the chasm. With my acrophobia, this gave me the creeps! My wife, too, can dangle her feet right next to a drop-off – not me! Thus I claimed that this daughter could not be my offspring – no way she could have my genes!

After that, our trip was nearing its end, except for the 72 mile Smoky Mountain Road of rough dirt and rock, returning through some wild and beautiful country to the Mormon settlement of Big Water near Lake Powell. It is called Smoky

Mountain because of some smoldering underground coal seams, ignited eons ago by lightning. Along this road are sights just begging to be explored. One of the smaller ones we did was an ancient Indian granary where natives had protected their grain harvest from rodents. At the end, I was glad that Nigel had to drive the 1,500 foot descent down the steeply dropping gravel road from the plateau down to Big Water – and home. –

Once more, this time five, Nigel, our leader, my wife Ute, Kathee and Vern, having had the good fortune to obtain permits through an online lottery, we were headed north the beginning of November 2008 to see the 'Wave', one of many wonderful rock formations.

The four hour drive from Prescott, AZ, to west of Page took us that afternoon to Mushroom Valley where sandstone columns stood, about 6-10 feet in diameter and twice that in height, protected from erosion by harder, darker colored capstones, giving them the appearance of giant mushrooms.

From there we drove and hiked to nearby Skylight Arch, located on a long promontory extending from a plateau. This is a most peculiar arch in that it does not project up from the plateau, but is formed by a hole, opening toward the cliff face. Not knowing where it was, one could walk right past it.

The following day we drove to Coyote Buttes South, and over 24 miles of rough dirt road to Cottonwood Cove. A one mile hike took us to one of the most fantastic sandstone formations I have ever seen! Rising from flat sandy scrubland, covered by a profusion of beautiful, feathery sage, were at least a dozen sandstone buttes of petrified sand dunes. On one of them we counted at least twelve discontinuities, called cross-bedding, where deposits had been eroded, then new ones added in the course of millions of years. Most amazing were the differential colorations of the deposits, some in straight layers, others in the most convoluted swirls imaginable. Between two buttes, we clambered up a 40 degree incline to reach a small plateau behind the buttes where, again and again, we found the most wonderful small and large rock formations.

Then it was off to Poverty Flat, an old cattle ranch where we had our sack lunch, then walked across the property to look for Moqui Marbles, round or oval black sandstone balls from millimeters to several centimeters in size, with a 'shell' quite high in iron content.

Thereafter, another dirt road brought us to White Pocket, which, actually, is not a pocket, but a sandstone rise with interesting formations. A sharp wind drove me back early to our Toyota Land Cruiser.

Our evenings were spent at a Page motel with an aperitif before dinner, then in a restaurant. This part could definitely not be called 'roughing it'!

On the last day, the Wave beckoned! This absolutely fantastic sandstone formation is located in the Coyote Buttes North area, just south of the Arizona/Utah border between Page and Kanab, requiring a three mile hike from the trailhead. Along a wash, up a hill, down into another wash, and up once more, we overlooked the magnificent countryside the American Southwest is so richly endowed.

And now, from the ridge we were standing on, we had to traverse along mountain slopes, all too often at 30 degrees, up and down, occasionally clambering up on all fours, slogging through sandy depressions to the Wave, in the far distance.

We were the second party to arrive to find, what appeared to be, three heavy tripod-equipped Japanese photographers taking pictures with a female model.

The Wave is not very large, maybe all in all about 30-40 meters, compared to some of the other larger formations we saw, but it makes up for it by its regular wavy, differentially-colored, sandstone bands and huge, convoluted pocketing.

Little by little, other permit holders 'dribbled in' and, after we had explored the inside and outside of the Wave, we made our difficult way back to our vehicle. Interestingly enough, homeward-bound felt shorter than hiking in.

Then it was home to Prescott. And for April 2009 it looks like we will be off again to see more of the magnificent countryside of Arizona and Utah, guided by friend Nigel Reynolds. For more photos and trips see his web site: BumpyRoadAdventures.com

Tanzania Redux

July 2015

Since childhood Africa has fascinated me. First it was the history of the colonial period. Then the animals, and finally my study of anthropology, whose findings have shown we are all Africans.

My first trip, at age twenty, took me via motorcycle from Germany to Libya and Egypt in an attempt, interrupted by the 1956 British/French attack on Egypt, to travel the length of the African continent all the way down to Cape Town. Imagine, King Idris, not Gaddafi, still ruled in Libya, and Nasser, in Egypt. I've survived them all.

It is important to point out that Africa is huge! It easily covers the area of the United States, all of China, and assorted smaller countries.

Then it took thirty years (a growing family and business intervened) to go to Tanzania and Kenya in 1985 on a safari with my wife. Our Tanzanian jump-off point was the town of Arusha which, at that time had a population of about sixty thousand to one hundred thousand. We went to the Serengeti, Ngorongoro, and up to the Mara, the tourist route, and were thoroughly impressed by the wildlife.

By this year, 2015, I had been on four sub-Saharan safaris and two Moroccan journeys, and felt a desire for a final safari to the part of the continent I love, East and southern Africa, where I had visited Zimbabwe, Namibia, Botswana, Zambia, the Cape, and Tanzania and Kenya.

Through the years I had stayed in loose touch with the Zambezi Safari Co., and after John Berry, its managing director included three of my Africa poems on his company blog, I felt like journeying with his organization. But I wanted to avoid the "madding crowd," not revisit what I had seen in Tanzania thirty years before. It never pays to revisit. It just isn't the same. Thus, my Zambezi Safari contact, Fi Thompson, suggested a safari through less crowded southern Tanzania, which I booked.

I traveled light, two long pants, five shirts, six pairs of socks, some underwear, a hat, some of which I wore, and some assorted knickknacks, which made up a small backpack of about 8 kg (18 lb) and a fanny pack. No checked luggage for me! My business class Delta flight from Phoenix via Detroit to Amsterdam and from there to Kilimanjaro airport in Tanzania ran into trouble. The Phoenix outbound flight was delayed by one and one-half hours due to a loose panel in the cabin. A rebooked flight would have arrived in Kilimanjaro three hours later, at 2300 hours (11 p.m.). Would my Nomad Safari pick-up wait for me? But, with a little endurance and luck, I made all my flights and arrived in Kilimanjaro on time at 2000 (8 p.m.). My Nomad pick-up man, Robert, was there, and assured me he would have waited!

Next came the night drive of about 60 km (40 miles) to Arusha. What traffic there was! I've never encountered as many speed bumps, and these on a main road. We arrived safely in Arusha where I was taken to the Onsea House for a day's rest and recuperation. It turned out to be a most pleasant place, with all the modern conveniences you'd expect in the U.S. or Europe, although the dirt road to it made me wonder what the place would really look like. The next day I got to know the owner, Axel Jenssen, a Flemish Belgian, and found during a long conversation that we both suffered from the same ailment – a slipped disc between L4/L5. It's a small world. To my shock I learned that Arusha's population was now estimated to be between one million and two million. I made Axel a gift of one of my poetry books.

Robert picked me up the following morning to take me to the Arusha airport, there to board a thirteen-seater Cessna. I was the sole passenger. A more than two hour flight, with a stopover at Tabora for refueling, brought us to the airstrip at the Katavi Reserve, where I was taken by safari vehicle to Chada camp. My pickup had to await the arrival of another plane while I waited in the car. The plane arrived, turned right in front of me to park, and I was covered in a cloud of dust raised by the prop wash. Ah well! Sammy, the manager of Chada camp was just a few seconds too late to cover me with a blanket.

Sammy was a tall, friendly, and helpful Massai. Eventually, departing for a half-hour drive to camp, a huge elephant crossed at the end of the airstrip, losing himself in the scrub. After many bumps – I was to experience lots more – we arrived at camp, where I was received, as is customary, with a warm wet towel to refresh face and hands, this together with a few friendly African smiles. I was taken to my ample rectangular tent with see-through walls, zipper enclosed, with attached washroom and outside bucket shower facility. The bucket had been filled with about 30 liters. I went for it. I hadn't removed all the soap yet when my water ran out. Ah well!

A little later a family group of Americans arrived. I am German, but have by now lived fifty years in North America and am at home in language and culture. The group's patriarch, ten years younger than I, carried the last name of Bull. We hit it off right away and "bulled" our way through the next four days. The group consisted of George, his wife, two children, a son-in-law, and the wife's sister. They were accompanied by friends, a white Kenyan couple, Charlie and Mouse. I never learned all their names but upon my departure George Bull and I hugged our good-bye never having bothered about addresses.

This casualness leads me to mention that I had no camera along, just a smart-phone, smarter than I, for a few pics, and no binocs. Long ago I decided to see what I can see. What I cannot, I don't. What I remember I will, and whatever else is fine to forget.

What I will never forget from my safaris is the call of the ring-necked dove. When I hear its sound in a nature show – without looking I know it is "Africa calling." Another call I became familiar with on an earlier safari in Zambia was put into words by our guide. It supposedly sounds like, "My father is dead, my mother is dead, and all my relatives, too." Now, in Tanzania, I could not recall the name of this dove but when I mentioned the above words, the Kenyan, Charlie, immediately said, "It's the emerald-spotted wood dove."

The tents looked out to a distant swamp through which meandered a seasonal river. A huge herd of cape buffalo, plenty of noisy hippos, elephants, and other creatures populated it. As I had picked up years earlier in Zimbabwe, I suggested a five dollar penalty for anyone calling a cape buffalo a water buffalo, something coming ever so easily. The cape buffalo is a dangerous wild beast while the water buffalo is a docile domesticated animal from Asia, its milk provides us with Mozarella cheese.

The first night the animals out there welcomed us with an ongoing concert. Twice I heard what sounded like a motorcycle. But who would ride a motorcycle through the African night? In the morning none of the guides had an explanation for the sound until one finally said it had come from a hippopotamus. The next nights were quiet. No motorcycles.

Through the following days we did game drives in open, tent-roofed safari vehicles, either Toyota Land Cruisers or British Land Rovers, seating up to seven people. But at most we were five, seeing plenty of elephants, zebras, giraffes, waterbuck, impalas (with their McDonald logo on their rear, called lion McDonalds), and other wildlife like the prolific impalas, and waterbuck, but were often haunted by pesky tsetse flies. Our guides made a valiant effort to track down the local lion pride but without luck. The not so little ellie (elephant) in the above picture challenged our safari vehicle but it was all bluff.

At last came a night drive, accompanied by a ranger with rifle, required only for night drives. Return and dinner were to be at 2030 (8:30 p.m. to 2100 (9 p.m.). On the way back the guides spotted a male lion and tracked him through the bushes for an eternity, losing and finding him again. They were totally engrossed and lost all sense of time. Finally he was gone. I should have put my foot down, for it was 2210 (10:10 p.m.) when we arrived back in camp. I had no more desire for food, was cold, and longed only for bed. There's this famous American saying. "Shit happens!" An ample breakfast of sausage, bacon, and scrambled eggs tasted good next morning.

How often have I recommended an African safari to my American friends. Few bit. Most imagined poor food, illness, and inconveniences. Well, at none of the many camps, present and past, have I had bad food or gotten sick. The creative variety of vegetables and salads, from leaf lettuce, beets, carrots and beans that are served is utterly amazing. Of course there are no steaks, but tasty morsels of meat, like chicken satés. One must imagine over what distances this produce and meat must be flown and trucked in. I complimented Sammy's cooks by telling him, again in jest – but all good jests carry an element of truth – that I would send a few chefs from my home town to his camp to learn tasty cooking! And all camps had a bar. Cooled wine and cold beer were always included for dinner, if so desired. And the table settings were equal, if not better than at "normal" American restaurants. The same was true for how the staff serve food and picked up tableware

Then came my farewell shower. This time I waited only briefly. When I stepped out, I saw a whole gang of vervet monkeys, a very naughty species, lined up drinking my shower water from the bucket. Subsequently I told Sammy in jest that this was probably the reason I had not had enough water for my first shower because these little monsters drank it. Sammy took me to the airstrip. Today I put one of my poetry books in the mail to him.

My next one and one-half hour flight was in a three-seater Cessna with me again being the only passenger going to the Ruaha Reserve. I enjoy flying in these small aircraft, which stay at a low altitude, enabling me to observe the changing landscape below. At one time we passed over a very large area of side-by-side circular clearings with a white dot at their center. I wondered what they were. Then it clicked. The white centers were termite mounds. The termites ate, and thus cleaned, the surrounding vegetation, producing the circles, as seen from above.

I was picked up at the airstrip by John from the Kigelia camp. Right away he complained about the many elephants bothering the settlement and area around the airstrip, which must be cleared of them before aircraft can land. Not that herds populate them, though. He told me that he was a Christian (Tanzania is about fifty-fifty Christian and Muslim) and that his grandfather had been an Afrikaner in South Africa from where his family emigrated to Tanzania.

The camp is named after *Kigelia africana*, the sausage tree which grows there. One night one of the 30 cm (1 ft) long, heavy sausage-like fruits, all suspended on a fiber string, crashed through the tarp of one of the safari vehicles.

Upon arrival, I relayed Sammy's greetings to Ken, the manager of Kigelia Camp. These folks all know each other, having moved among camps, even all the way north to the Serengeti. I was put into tent #1, the most remote, but was told that they would move me to a closer tent. My response was that I would be fine where I was. I made it a habit to tell every new camp manager of my abilities and disabilities, including that I was pushing eighty years. Lo and behold, this brought me a tad more consideration. Isn't it true that Africans revere age? If there were only other benefits to advanced age.

I received a tasty lunch after which I moved into tent #1 where I dispersed all my necessities in the washroom, put away my clothes, and dumped my dirty laundry into the hamper to be washed. Then I lay down on the big king-size bed and promptly fell asleep. A bit later I was awakened by steps I thought were coming from outside, maybe asking me to come for tea. Looking up I faced a huge tusker covering almost the entire broadside of my see-through abode at a distance of about a meter (yard) away, happily munching the plentiful greenery. Familiar with such encounters, I admired the creature. A little later I walked down to the camp's center and reported my meeting. Then it was off on a game drive. Upon our return, I found that the camp staff had moved me to tent #5, closer to the central facilities. The pesky elephant had worried them. My dispersed belongings had been transferred and placed where they belonged in my new "home." Still, the huge beast kept wandering through camp for the next few days and had to be shooed repeatedly.

Again, there was plenty of wildlife to see on the game drives – giraffes, elephants, hippos, crocs, impalas, elands, and waterbucks. Waterbucks have a white ring on their posterior. The story goes that their progenitor sat on a freshly painted toilet seat and was marked with this ring. What I did not get to see in any of the camps were ostriches, cheetahs, and wildebeest. Regrettably, rhinos have all been poached. And a leopard our guide spotted could only be seen by him and through the camera tele-objectives of my fellow-travelers, and thus not by me. Night drives, with powerful light beams projected from the vehicles, often showed more animals, or different ones than day drives. It was on these, when we saw hyenas, warthogs, porcupines, genets, bat-eared foxes, together with the gamut of the "regular" creatures. The King of Beasts shown above, Simba in Suaheli, was head of a small pride with cubs.

My favorite guide was Hussein. His nickname was Saddam, but I never called him that. Obviously, he was Muslim. With him I learned that these guides attend a two-year wildlife college where they learn the basics of guiding. All too often a foreigner may gain the impression that the local people have limited education. Some of this impression is due to the fact that their primary language is Suaheli, the lingua franca of eastern Africa. Their English is thus not perfect; however underneath often dwells an astounding knowledge of the environment, if not the world at large.

The first evening I heard the distant roar of a lion challenging another distant pride. At five o'clock next morning we were awakened by a deafening roar from the wash beside the tents, answered distantly by the other pride. None of us needed another wake-up call!

In camp and on the game drives I made friends with a British couple, Harry and Heather. I learned they were commercial mediators. I had never heard of this occupation before but it must be very profitable for, although somewhat younger than I, they had traveled the world, and were also old African hands. They were "birders" and checked off every bird they saw in a book. From the guides here I learned that, as a group of lions is called a "pride," a group of giraffes is called a "tower of giraffes," and an assemblage of elephants, a "promenade of elephants." Giraffes sometimes gather their young in a group, guarded by an adult. Such a group is called a "kindergarten of giraffes." And here, on this game drive, I saw my first lion in daylight.

On my last day a Belgian family arrived and we looked forward to meeting afterwards in the next camp. Their twenty-one-year-old daughter, Jill, eagerly down-loaded her Belgian college test scores via Internet that evening. She had been unable to obtain them prior to their departure.

"When will I get my washed clothes back?" I asked on the eve of my last day's stay. "Well," Ken said, "you put your dirty clothes on a shelf, not into the hamper." "Oh, no," I responded. "They went immediately in the hamper." Shucks, they had transferred all my belongings, but had failed to check the hamper. Thus a rush ensued and next morning I had my clothes washed and ironed, if still a tad moist. We had a good laugh about it. That darn elephant!

Next morning my flight took me to the biggest game reserve in Africa, the Selous. It is named after the British big-game hunter, Frederick Courtney Selous, who joined the British forces in WWI and, as captain of his attachment, was killed near there in a skirmish with German troops and buried nearby. The reserve is located in southeast Tanzania where a lot of poaching is going on. I rarely saw an elephant there. They shyly stayed in the brush and forest environment and came out only at night.

The ride from the airstrip to the Sand River Selous camp was over sometimes atrocious roads. Oddly though, the many bumps did not affect my twice-operated-on L4/L5 spine. The twenty-year-old lodge facilities were luxurious, appointed with comfortable chairs and sofas, well-made coffee tables, a well-stocked bar, some tables decorated with the skulls of wild animals. No elephants, though! The lodge, close by, overlooks the Rufiji River. Crocs and hippos populated its waters and

202

banks. I was greeted by an attractive young couple, Ilse and Jeff, she from South Africa, he a Scott. Jeff told about his intention next year to travel the Rufiji its entire length to the Indian Ocean, a distance of about 110 km (70 miles) as the crow flies. Talking about his planned adventure, I asked him what he figured the actual distance would be with all the bends and false arms and he estimated "about 220 km (140 miles)." I told him: "Were I a few decades younger I would love to accompany you." He thought that the Rufiji had never before been traveled that distance.

At the camp I was accommodated in their closest, well, what to call it? My large, fixed-site A-frame abode, sturdily-built, with a thatched-roof, was open to the river with a view through the trees. By night a king-size bed was enclosed by mosquito netting, all arranged by staff. I shared the bathroom with a little lizard by night. By day it hunted on the doorsteps. The bathroom had a "waterfall shower. And, of course, this facility, as in all the previous camps, sported a flush toilet.

In conversations with Ilse, I made her a gift of my second poetry collection, *Pondering What Is*. This, plus my traveling solo, gave me the pleasure of dining twice with the pleasant couple. As in Chada, I went here for a relatively brief game walk with Jeff. I had voiced my apprehension about the walk taxing me, which it had done in Chada. So they arranged to have me picked up while the Belgian couple continued, minus their daughter, who'd also had enough, were picked up later at a designated spot. Among many other interesting stories, Jeff related that on one of his ventures, a participant was gored in the rear by a buffalo. "What did you do?" I asked. "Well, we took him back to camp and I fixed him up with a couple of stitches." Very comforting, I thought, to have a surgeon with a rifle along.

A boat ride took the Belgians, Karl, wife Madeleine, Jill, and me up the Rufiji to "the Gorge," where the usually broad and sandy river narrows substantially. Still, the occasional croc could be spotted in the narrows. Our guide set up a hearty breakfast of pancakes, sausage, bacon, yoghurt, wraps with lettuce and chicken, plus pineapple and watermelon slices, on the boulders, after which we fished, with little luck, for Tiger fish. On the trip we saw more hippos – I estimated a hundred. When our boat approached them, those on land all dashed for the water, especially when their pod included babies.

Except for one day the maximum number of guests at each of the camps did not exceed ten. It was always a congenial "crowd." And at all camps one of the first questions the guides asked me was, "Which animal do you like best?" After a little hesitation my response was, "I like them all." But I must admit, I like elephants most.

All good things had to come to an end. Later I took it easy, lazing about camp, reading the life story of Lettow-Vorbeck, the commander of the German colonial troops in Tanganyika. Tanzania was a German colony until 1918. He gave the British the run-around and surrendered with his German and native Askaris only after Germany had accepted the armistice. He was respected by friend and foe. In 1928 Germany paid the Tanganyikan Askaris/soldiers their missed pay, ten years after the war!

At Sand River I was told that the Dar es Salaam International Airport, my next destination on the way home, had no business class lounge to relax in. Upon my arrival at the Dar domestic airport a Nomad representative awaited me holding a sign with my name, to drive me the short distance to the international airport. I arrived at 1300 (1 p.m.) and discovered an upstairs air-conditioned restaurant. For my lunch I ordered a *Bavaria* beer, thinking I'd try something "new." It turned out to be alcohol-free and sweetish. So I ordered a Heineken instead. And the chicken of my meal really tasted like chicken, not like the cage-reared US type. Alas, after two hours I felt I could no longer linger in this cool place and had to face the Dar heat. I had learned from the restaurant porter that no passenger was allowed inside the terminal before 2000 (8 p.m.). So I sat on the stairs or chairs for over five hours, wandering with the wandering sun. In time, I talked with two other business class travelers also waiting to get into the cool and away from the chaos and heat in front of the terminal. By 2030 (8:30 p.m.) we were let in and, wonder of wonders, there was a cool airline lounge. Had we only known or been told!

The KLM flight took off on time. But it turned out that my reclining seat had a disfunction – no proper footrest. Business class seats differ among airlines. I tried to find comfort but finally told the purser that my seat felt like it had been made by Torquemada, the Grand Inquisitor. I soon moved to a functioning vacant seat. Always trying to make the best of it, I told the two female flight attendants and the purser about my African exploits, also my age, and had some nice chats that long night.

Then, after Amsterdam, where everyone was most thoroughly checked, came my US-destination, Salt Lake City, and from there home to Phoenix. I am proud to say that I succeeded in smuggling my always handy, tiny Swiss Army Knife through all checkpoints.

I had spent my last evening In Tanzania sitting alone on the terrace at the Sand River Selous, looking across the Rufiji River into the settling dusk, pondering my experiences. In the course of my trip, Jupiter, which the first night had shone a bit above shiny Venus, had gradually wandered ever closer and had finally arrived below Venus. I sketched a poem about this final experience and put it into verse at home. Here it is:

Let me close on an elegiac note.

As I said at the beginning of my story: "I love Africa," her east and south, the often sere lands, her people, her profusion of animals, her ancient history, our human history. If my

health and age would permit it, I would go once more. It never becomes dull, although the exciting impressions of my first passage through Tanzania and Kenya simply cannot be repeated.

Made in the USA
Monee, IL
05 April 2021